ACT NOW!

ACT
NOW!

A Step-by-Step Guide
on How to Become a
Working Actor

PETER JAZWINSKI

THREE RIVERS PRESS

NEW YORK

Published by Three Rivers Press, New York, New York.
Member of the Crown Publishing Group, a division of
Random House, Inc.
www.randomhouse.com

THREE RIVERS PRESS and the Tugboat design are registered
trademarks of Random House, Inc.

Printed in the United States of America

Design by Susan Hood

Library of Congress Cataloging-in-Publication Data
Jazwinski, Peter, 1964–
Act now! : a step-by-step guide on how to become a working
actor / Peter Jazwinski.—1st. ed.
1. Acting—Vocational guidance—California—Los Angeles.
2. Acting.   3. Motion picture acting.   I. Title.
PN2055.J43 2003
791.43'028'023—dc21   2003004999

ISBN 1-4000-4862-1

10   9   8   7   6   5   4   3   2   1

First Edition

To Norman Sturgis, Sandra Mayer, and Katherine Jenner,
who showed me the joy of creative expression

ACKNOWLEDGMENTS

I'D like to acknowledge the following people and thank them for their strong support.

My agent, Frank Scatoni, of Venture Literary was the principal player in getting this project done. His guidance and encouragement were instrumental in moving these ideas out of my head and onto the page.

Pete Fornatale, my editor at Random House, did a magnificent job of helping me sort out what was really important and necessary. Pete picked up where Frank left off, and it was a true pleasure to work with both of these fine wordsmiths.

Dorianne Steele at Random House, who guided me through the publishing process with great efficiency and patience. Jennifer O'Connor, for designing such a beautiful cover. Laurie McGee, who went through the manuscript and made all the necessary corrections. Your skills are awe-inspiring.

My wife, Cloe, and my daughter, Storm, who are always there.

Last, I'd like to thank all those aspiring actors who found me through the Internet and kept asking such excellent and curious questions. Your desire and excitement inspire me every day.

CONTENTS

Introduction

I'M THE ONE WHO THINKS
YOU CAN MAKE IT

I ONLY read book introductions if they're less than five pages, so I'm keeping this short. I don't want to waste your time with a lot of explanations. Instead, I want to help you get started on your quest to become an actor.

If you tell someone you want to be an investment banker, you're met with a smile and well wishes. If you tell someone you want to sell advertising, they'll say, "I hear there's great money in advertising." However, if you tell someone that you want to be an actor, you're written off as a dreamer and told to do something more realistic—whatever that means. What if Tom Cruise had decided to do something more realistic?

If you're an unknown actor in Hollywood and you tell someone about your dream, you're usually met with a snicker. "Good luck," they'll say sarcastically. "Oh, another actor. Where do you wait tables?"

The glory of being in the spotlight is as indescribable as it is desirable. It's one of the driving forces behind every actor, whether they admit it or not. Those who don't achieve fame or notoriety can become very jealous and bitter. When they hear that someone else is trying to make it, they vent their frustration by saying, "You'll never make it. Be more realistic." What they're really doing is expressing their own fear of failure.

If you haven't encountered this yet in your life, then start telling people that you want to become an actor and you'll see what I mean. Come to Hollywood and start telling the waiters, cab drivers, store clerks, and pizza delivery guys that you want to be an actor. They'll practically laugh in your face.

I know how much courage and determination it takes to try to make it in Hollywood, and that's one of the reasons I wrote this book. I'm not a famous actor, but I have a lot of experience that I can share. I've acted in movies, on TV, and onstage. I've written plays, films, and books. I've managed actors and taught classes. I know what it takes and what you're going to have to do if you want to give it a shot.

I once asked an actor who'd been in the business for more than twenty years how I could go about becoming an actor. He stammered a bit and giggled slightly before muttering, "Well, you don't just *become* an actor. I mean, uh, there's a lot of stuff." So I asked him again more pointedly if he could give me the general steps. He started a few sentences before finally agreeing that I should ". . . get an agent." I tried one more time to ask if he would recommend any particular path. He cut me off by saying, "What kind of a question is that? *How do I become an actor?*"

The fellow with whom I had spoken had been an actor, writer, producer, director, and stagehand in Hollywood and New York for twenty years. That's the problem many beginning actors face. There is no end to the "expert" advice about agents, head-shots, résumés, and interviews, but nobody has ever put together a comprehensive, step-by-step plan that, if followed, could put an aspiring actor in the best possible position to get an agent and to get acting auditions. That's what *Act Now!* does, and anyone who follows the steps faithfully will accomplish just that. I know, because I followed all of the steps in this plan and got auditions, a Screen Actors Guild (SAG) card, and a speaking part in a scene with Jim Carrey in his famous film *The Mask*. It wasn't an accident. It was the direct result of persistently following all of the steps outlined in *Act Now!*

Before all that happened, though, I was just like you. I wanted to break into acting, but I didn't really know what to do. I had heard about headshots and agents, and I had talked to some people and read some books, but I wasted a lot of time once I moved to Los Angeles because I didn't really have a systematic approach. Oh, and I also got scammed and misled, so if that's ever happened to you, don't feel bad. If it hasn't happened to you, you're lucky, and you're now going to benefit from the mistakes I made when I was trying to figure it all out.

I have worked with actors who have come to me from all over the country with no experience at all. Then three months or a year later, they have an agent and they're out auditioning instead of sitting at home dreaming. They're doing the same thing that every actor who ever made it did. The only difference is that with my help, they don't waste the first five years of their career fumbling around and getting scammed as they try to figure out how to get started.

I want to be that one person in your life who thinks it's fantastic that you want to become an actor. I want to be that one person who says that you *can* make it. I want to be that buoy of hope in a sea of pessimism that you can cling to for truthful advice and honest encouragement. I am not going to infect you with my own fears; instead, I'd like to inspire you with my own hope and well wishes.

If you have the courage to follow the steps in this book, then you'll have a chance to make it. Hollywood needs new faces every year. There's no law that says the next new face can't be yours. So the next time you tell someone that you want to be an actor, and they ridicule you, just remember that there's one guy out there who thinks you can make it. I'll not scoff at you. I'm absolutely cheering for your success.

I

WHAT DID YOU DO TODAY TO ADVANCE YOUR ACTING CAREER?

Do you ever ask yourself that question? Think about that for a second. Other than picking up this book, did you do anything else today to advance your acting career? If you have an answer for that today, will you have an answer for that question tomorrow? Here's the first secret about succeeding: The more often you have an answer for that question, the faster you're going to succeed. Write this question down. *What did you do today to advance your acting career?* The answers to that question will be the most important information you ever learn as an actor.

If you can't answer that question each day or each week because you're lazy, then there isn't a book or coach in the world who can help you. If, however, you can't answer that question because you simply don't know what to do, then you're in luck, because I'm going to teach you exactly what you need to do to advance your acting career. It won't matter how old you are, where you live, or how much experience you have. As long as you can follow the steps of this book, you'll have a good answer for that question each day, and you'll be on your way to becoming an actor.

Your overall goal

I'm sure you have some kind of goal in mind for yourself. Maybe you want to be a major movie star or you want to be on a hit television show. That's great, and in the world of show business, anything is possible. Let's call that your "Overall Goal." Jim Carrey has often talked about the night he drove his car up into the Hollywood Hills before he made it big and wrote a check to himself for $26 million. He said that his goal was to make that much money doing movies. Years later, he got paid exactly that amount. What's your overall goal? Go ahead and write it down. Keep it in mind and I'll show you how to reach it.

If you ask a major star like Brad Pitt, Nicole Kidman, John Travolta, or Meryl Streep how they became famous, they probably won't tell you that they called a big talent agent and the next day they got paid millions of dollars to star in a box-office smash. They might be able to do that now, but that's not how they started and that's not how you're going to start. First they learned how to act. Then they built up some experience. Then, based on that little bit of experience, they got an agent. Once they got an agent, they got some better roles. Once they got the better roles, they got a better agent. Once they got a better agent, they got the really big roles and the really big money that goes along with it. That's how it works. It's okay to have really big goals, but you must know where to start and what to do, and that's what I'm going to explain.

Your main goal

Once you've established your overall goal, it's time to talk about your *main goal.* Do you know what your main goal is? Let me tell you what it is. You should write this down, too. Your main goal is *to put yourself in the best possible position to get an audition.* That might not sound very glamorous, but that's the real secret to succeeding as an actor. This goal is more important than learning the craft of acting itself and I can prove it.

Let's say there are ten actors at an audition, and they're all pretty good. They aren't the best, but they're okay. Maybe some of them are really bad. Some don't even have any training, but it's the last audition and the casting director has to pick one of them. Also on that day, there's a super actor who nobody's ever heard of and he's at home watching soaps on television. Who is going to get the part? Obviously, the great actor at home isn't going to get picked because he's not even at the audition. One of the ten actors standing in front of the casting director is going to get picked. That brings up a very important point. A casting director can only cast people who show up at auditions. That's why your main goal has to be to get an audition. The more you do it, the more chances you have.

It's not your right as a citizen of the world to get an audition for something. If you want an audition, you have to go find it. If you have an agent, then your agent has to find it. Remember that. Nobody just calls you out of the blue and says, "Hi, I understand you've always wanted to be a movie star. Come to this audition today." You have to find auditions. The good news is that they happen every day, and I'll teach you how to find them.

Think of a television show like *Friends*. There was a time when all of the cast members had to audition for those parts. Casting directors had to choose the six cast members. Those six actors are very talented and entertaining, but they never would have been chosen for those parts if they didn't find that audition. Just like you are never going to get a part if you don't find an audition. So even though you have to be an entertaining and creative person to actually act, you have to be a very determined and persistent person to find those auditions that will allow you to show your talents. It can be done, but you have to start from the beginning and that brings us to your daily goal.

Your daily goal

To reach your overall goal, you have to reach your main goal first. The only way to reach your main goal is to complete a daily goal. Your daily goal is to do whatever is available to you right now in your town. Throughout this book you're going to learn about headshots, training, demo reels, auditions, casting directors, and much more. The way to keep moving forward is to keep doing whatever you can.

I often get e-mails from children in small towns who say things like, "Pete, there are no theaters here and I'm too young to travel, but I really want to be in the movies. Can you get me an agent?" The answer is no.

Getting an agent is not what's available to this person right now in her situation. Therefore she shouldn't focus on that goal. Instead she should try something like gathering her friends and performing a play in her backyard. That might not be what she wants to hear, but that's what's available to her right now and that's what she needs to do. Once she's learned to act, has gotten a headshot, has collected some credits on her résumé, and has moved to a bigger city, then she can focus on the step of looking for an agent because the opportunity will then be available.

At the end of each chapter, I'll list some daily goals so that you can keep track of the things that will take you to your overall goal. The way to complete these daily goals is to constantly ask yourself this question, "What did you do today to advance your acting career?" If you can keep finding answers to that question, then you'll be on your way. If you can't find an answer, then you'll know that you're not doing anything and you need to focus on the next attainable step.

The only way you fail is by not trying

If you are fortunate enough to audition for a casting director, and you don't get the part, you did not fail. That's right. If you go to an audition, and you perform, and you do not get cast, you did not fail. The reason I say that is because once you audition, you have no control over whether or not they pick you. They could say no because of your hair, your mouth, your height, your weight, your glasses, your shoes, the way you look or sound next to the other actors, or any other reason. However, they could also say yes for any reason as well. Actors never really know why they do or don't get cast for something, and every major actor has been turned down multiple times before he or she got that first big role. My point is that you have no control over whether or not you get picked. You do have control over whether or not you make it to the audition in the first place, and that's why one of your main goals is to put yourself in the best possible position to get an audition. The person who fails is the actor who simply *wishes* he were at an audition, because he is definitely not going to get cast. The person who succeeds is the one who makes it to the audition. Which one are you going to be?

I'll tell you more about the casting process in a later chapter, but right now I want you to realize that if you find yourself in an audition, then you have already achieved your main goal. Most actors never get that far because they're too concerned with their overall goal of being famous. Think of your overall goal as putting the flag on top of Mount Everest. You don't start at the top and stick the flag in the snow on day one. You have to start at the bottom and work your way up. As long as you're taking steps each day, you're working toward that goal, but if you stop walking and spend all your time dreaming about what it's like at the top, then you'll never get there.

Landing an agent is a similar process. If you or your picture winds up in the hands of a talent agent, then you have succeeded in completing another important step toward getting better auditions. If the agent doesn't want to work with you, you have not failed, because you can't control that part. The failure is the actor who sits at home watching *Seinfeld* reruns saying, "Man, if only I could meet an agent, I'd be a star." The successful actor is the one who gets her picture into an agent's hand, because at least she's giving herself a chance to succeed.

Wishing is not enough

I once heard a writer say, "Writers never fail; they just give up." The same could be said about actors. I live and work in Los Angeles, and I can't tell you how many truly funny, talented, and gifted actors I have met who have not done one thing to get past, "I want to be an actor." They work as bartenders, waitresses, telemarketers, and production assistants, and they bad-mouth all the successful people with awful words like, "Ah, that Tom Cruise can't act," or "Julia Roberts has no talent." Can you imagine such stupidity? Actually, it's not stupidity—it's jealousy. Tom and Julia got where they are today because they worked their butts off and never gave up.

Believe it or not, at one time Tom and Julia were in the same position as you. That's right. Tom Cruise was not born with a long résumé, a great headshot, and a high salary. When she started out, Julia Roberts didn't have one acting credit. She had to audition for her first role at some point in her life. Tom and Julia were not sitting in their living rooms watching television, wishing they were famous, and then one day, someone called them up and said, "Do you want to be a movie star?" They had to go to acting classes. They had to get pictures done. They had to audition, and they got beat out for parts by other actors. Of course today they're very famous and they're both considered excellent actors, but that wouldn't have happened if they didn't try. It won't happen to you, either, if you don't try.

I'm not saying that all you have to do is try and you'll be as famous as Tom Cruise or Julia Roberts. What I'm saying is that the first step is entirely up to you. You can't just read books about acting or go to movies or surf websites. Here's a cold, hard fact: You will never become an actor unless you actually engage yourself in a systematic plan toward reaching your goal.

I have yet to read a news story about a girl who was just sitting at her job one day and all of a sudden became a movie star. Occasionally you'll hear an old story about how some actor from the 1950s was working as a cashier or a waitress and got discovered by a talent scout, but if you check your calendar, you'll see that those days are long gone. Sometimes we read about the latest overnight success who just got a role in a movie or a television show. More often than not that same actor will laugh at such a statement and say, "Where were they when I was back in Indiana doing theater for free and trying to save money to get to Hollywood?" The truth is that it just doesn't happen without your making an effort.

Regardless of what you wish to achieve in life, if you want to have huge success, then you're going to have to muster a huge amount of desire. Nowhere is this more relevant than in the world of show business.

What kind of person succeeds as an actor?

Do you ever watch television or a movie and think, "I could do that"? Those actors were once in the same position as you. They simply wanted to act. So how come they succeeded? It's all about persistence and determination. Let's look at a tale of two actors and see what we can learn. We'll call these actors Kyle and Karen.

Meet Kyle. Kyle's funny, talented, and good-looking. Everyone tells him, "You should be an actor." He says, "Yeah, I know, I gotta get some headshots some day." His day starts around noon when he gets up and finds the aspirin to cure his hangover. He drinks his coffee and talks to his mom on the phone while he watches daytime television. He meets a buddy at the gym around 2:00 P.M. and goes through a light workout while talking about the action at the bar last night. He goes home and changes and catches a nap before heading off to his bartender job where he works until 2:00 A.M. At the bar, he's hilarious. He has a few drinks, he does his Jay Leno impersonation, and all his friends say, "You're funny, you should be an actor." He says, "Yeah, I know, I'm gonna get some headshots next week."

When he gets home, Kyle flips through the channels on television. Even though he doesn't make much money, he has the full cable package. He doesn't know much about cooking so he eats out a lot. He looks through the bills on his coffee table and sees that he's behind on two credit cards. "Ah, don't worry about it," he thinks. "As soon as I make it big, I'll have plenty of money to take care of that." For now, though, he has to call his mom and ask her to send him some more money. He thinks Tom Cruise has no talent. He thinks Julia Roberts is just a pretty girl who can't act. He thinks he's funnier than Drew Carey, and he thinks that Hollywood talent agents don't know anything about acting. He also thinks that most movies suck and he could write a much better movie if he could just find the time to do it. He's not famous because he's too busy.

If you've ever lived in Los Angeles or New York, then you've probably met someone just like Kyle. There are thousands of actors like him. At least they call themselves actors. They were those really funny, good-looking class clowns from high school who were going to become movie stars. All they thought they had to do was move to Hollywood. If you don't live near the city, then you might think I'm joking. I'm not. These are the guys who give acting and show business a bad name. Let's look at another example.

Meet Karen. Karen is also talented. She has average looks and nobody ever tells her she should be an actor. She tells everyone else she's an actor. She gets up at 8:00 each morning and checks her e-mail, reads the entertainment headlines and the trade magazines, and checks her acting websites for leads. She opens her appointment book and sees that she needs to mail two headshots to the production company that is making a film about a female softball team, because she used to play softball in high school in Texas, where she grew up. The phone rings and it's a local college student who placed a casting notice on the Internet for a short film he's making. Karen sent him her photo two weeks ago and now he wants to meet her for an audition. She marks it down in her appointment book for tomorrow.

Next, she mails ten letters to talent agents, along with her headshot, asking for representation. She counts her headshots to make sure that she has enough for the rest of the month. Then she practices the monologue she got out of a book of famous plays. After lunch, Karen goes down to a local theater where open auditions are being held for an original play. She sits in the lobby for an hour before she is called. When it's her turn, she performs her monologue as best she can and thanks the director for her chance. Later in the day, she meets with friends at their favorite coffee shop where they snack, gossip, exchange leads, and have a good time. That night, Karen goes to her job at the restaurant where she works as a hostess. Before going to bed, she looks at herself in the mirror and says, "What did you do today to advance your acting career?"

Over the course of time, who is more likely to get an acting job or a talent agent? Is Kyle going to get work? He has the looks. He has the "talent." He's hilarious. He's handsome. Everyone says he's a natural-born actor. Why hasn't he been discovered?

Why is Karen more likely to get work? Is she so talented? Is she so great-looking? Does she have some secret connection? I hope now that you're starting to see what "talent" really is. Karen is more likely to get work because she's putting herself in the best possible position to succeed. Remember that there is no guarantee of success or stardom. Karen might not ever get cast in anything and she might not go any further than Kyle, but it's also possible that her next audition could be for a hit television show that makes her as famous as Jennifer Aniston.

Here's the most exciting and important question: Is Karen doing anything that you can't do? *No.* You can do the exact same thing as Karen if you want to because I'll teach you how to do all those things. What I can't teach you, though, is how to find the discipline and the courage to do it. Karen does all this because she finds it in her heart to work hard. Maybe she has great parents. Maybe she had a great teacher in high school who inspired her to work hard. Maybe she just really wants to become an actor more than anything else. Kyle sleeps all day because he can't find the energy to do anything else. The bottom line is that Karen truly wants to be an actor. Kyle just wants to be famous. Karen focuses on her main goal and that puts her in a position to possibly reach her overall goal. Kyle daydreams about his overall goal and that gets him nowhere.

Kyle did do one thing right. He moved to Hollywood. Some people never even make that step. However, just making the move doesn't mean a thing if you don't take the next step. What I want you to learn from this story is that it takes work on your part. If you don't have the determination that Karen has, then you shouldn't even bother taking the first step. I also want you to know that you don't have to live in Hollywood or New York to get started. You'll probably want to move to one of those cities eventually, but when you're starting out it doesn't matter where you live.

What about all the competition?

"You can't be an actor. You'll be competing with thousands of actors for the same job." Did you ever hear anyone say something like that? I hear it all the time. Let me translate it for you so that you understand what these people are really saying: *I'm too scared to try anything that courageous, so I don't want you to try.* Don't let anybody impose their fears on you. "Don't try to be an actor," they say. "You'll just be disappointed if you don't make it." I hope you always ignore cowards like this. Let me be the first one who encourages you to go for it. You have nothing to lose. Life is too short not to try something daring. If you don't make it as an actor, you'll still be a remarkable person because you tried.

Many people say that acting is too competitive. Here's a secret that these people don't know because they've never actually tried to make it as an actor. There is very little competition. In all the auditions I've been to, I've never seen more than ten to fifteen individuals at any casting call. Sometimes you see hundreds or thousands at an open call, but those are rare. I'm talking about a real audition where actors perform before the casting director or producer. There are never more than a few people there. Where are the thousands of actors that you're supposedly competing against? I'll tell you where they are. They're over at Kyle's house getting drunk watching the Super Bowl and yelling, "Dude, when I make it big, I'm gonna fly all of us to the Super Bowl. Pass me the chips."

Those thousands of actors you're competing against are not serious. They want to be actors, but they're meandering through the maze of show business without a clue. People like Karen, on the other hand, a girl who is focused, determined, serious, and following all the steps that I describe in this book, is one of those ten to twenty people who actually makes it to an audition. Out of those twenty, ten are the wrong type and two can't act. You're only competing against eight other actors. If you go on enough auditions, those are pretty good odds. But you'll never get those odds if you don't get on a program and stick to it.

What happens if I don't make it?

"But, Pete, what if I don't make it?" Let's think about that for a moment. Suppose you do all this work and never "make it." There are many different definitions for "making it," but we won't go into that. Well, you'll either continue trying until the day you die, or you'll try something else, just like you're doing something else right now. The difference will be that you'll feel good about yourself because you gave it your best effort. You won't be a failure because failure is not whether or not you become a movie star. Failure is simply *not trying*.

When I graduated from high school, I wanted to be an Olympic athlete and compete in the decathlon. I moved to Philadelphia and began training with a man named Jim Woodring, who went on to represent the United States in the 1984 Olympics. When I told friends what I was doing, some of them laughed and said I was crazy. Others wished me well. After about four months of training, I realized that I simply didn't have the gifts it would take to compete at a world-class level. I stopped training and went on to do other things. When I look back on it, I'm proud that I gave it a try. Sometimes I laugh when I think how naïve I was, but I never waste one second thinking, "Gee, I wonder if I could've gone to the Olympics?"

It's very possible that you could go through all the steps of this book only to find out that once you get to the audition, you never get picked for the part. Maybe you'll get rejected at your first audition and then you'll quit. Maybe you'll be like James Franco, costar of *Spiderman,* and you'll get rejected at your first hundred auditions. Maybe you'll quit then. It won't make you happy, but it's still better than not trying and having to wonder your whole life about what might have been.

I can teach you how to put yourself in a position to succeed, but only you can decide if you have what it takes to follow through with it. For my plan to work, you need to be willing to commit to it. Challenge yourself to say, "This is the time that I'm actually going to do it." Stop and say it to yourself right now. If you can't do it, then just put this book down and forget about acting.

Let's look at Kyle again. How do you think he feels? He'll have to go through life knowing that there was something he wanted to do very badly, but he never had the courage or the discipline to genuinely give it a shot. That's a tough pill to swallow. You have one life and one chance to be an actor. If your biggest concern is what happens if you don't make it, then you don't really want to be an actor. I'm not going to mislead you and say that it's easy and that you'll become a star if you simply read this book. What I will say is that you will never make it if you don't try, and this book teaches you absolutely everything you need to know so that you *can* try.

People who really want to be actors or doctors or carpenters or anything else don't worry about what will happen if they fail. They only think about how to succeed. That's the kind of mindset you need to have if you want to "make it."

A new definition of "talent"

Let me tell you the story of an actor named Elizabeth Peña. Elizabeth Peña thought she would be right for a part in the 1985 film *Down and Out in Beverly Hills*. She asked an agent to submit her for the role, but the agent said she wasn't pretty enough. Elizabeth then went to the gates of Disney and convinced a security guard to take her demo reel to the casting director. The casting director called her and said she would be perfect for the part. After that, Elizabeth went on to land roles in *La Bamba, Jacob's Ladder, Blue Steel, The Waterdance, Free Willy 2, Lone Star, Rush Hour,* and *Strangeland*.

When you're a famous actor like Al Pacino, Angelina Jolie, or Russell Crowe, your talent is measured by your performance on the screen. These actors are considered talented because they deliver creative, compelling performances. For a beginning actor like yourself, however, "talent" is defined as the ability to put yourself in a position to succeed. The most talented actor is not the guy with the best looks or the best voice. The most talented actor is the girl who is able to get her picture into the hands of someone who can help her. Think again about Elizabeth Peña. What was her talent? At first, her talent was her ability to get her demo reel into the hands of the casting director. There might have been another actor who could act better or was better looking than her, but while she was out partying with her friend Kyle, Elizabeth was busy getting the part.

Your recipe for success

Act Now! will show you exactly what to do every step of the way. You hardly have to think. All you have to do is provide the courage and determination to follow the plan. "But, Pete, if that's true, then everyone would do it." Everyone won't succeed at acting because it requires too much work. It's much easier to lie on the couch and watch television than it is to try to get *on* television.

If you are talented, you will find that determination. If you are not talented, you will not find that determination. Whichever path you take is entirely up to you. If you think you have the courage and determination, then read this entire book and learn how to succeed. If you ever find yourself doubting your desire, then come back to this chapter and reread these words of encouragement. You will meet those who will laugh at you, who will discourage you, and who will doubt you. I, on the other hand, truly want you to succeed. I want you to read this book and find the courage to follow the plan and find your dream. You can do it. The only question remaining is "Will you do it?"

ACTION POINTS

- From now on, think of "talent" as your ability to put yourself in a position to succeed.
- Differentiate between your overall goal, your main goal, and your daily goal.
- Your desire is the most important factor in your success.
- Wishing and dreaming are not enough. You have to actually follow the steps if you want to make it.

DAILY GOALS

I'll give you two daily goals to start with. The first is to continue reading this book. The second is to write down this phrase: "What did you do today to advance your acting career?" Say that phrase out loud every day. The daily goals that I'll give you from now on will provide the answers to that question. The more times you can come up with an answer, the faster you'll reach your main goal. The faster you reach your main goal, the faster you'll reach your overall goal.

2

HOW ACTORS GET CAST

Now that you've made up your mind to become an actor and you understand what kind of dedication is involved, it's time to begin actually pursuing your dream. In the next chapter you'll discover Your Acting Plan, which is the step-by-step plan for finding an agent and getting auditions. Before you read that plan though, you need to learn how the casting process works.

I would say that 90 percent of the questions I am asked by new actors could be answered simply by understanding how the actor, the agent, the manager, and the casting director all interact. It's common for actors to make naïve mistakes when they're starting out. But time is not on your side in show business, so the faster you figure out how the system works, the better off you'll be.

Here are the top five most common questions that I answer on my website every week. See if you have similar concerns.

1. Can you please tell me how I can audition for *Spiderman 2* (or any major movie)?
2. How do I audition for a TV show?

3. I'm making a trip to Los Angeles for two weeks and I'd like to go to some auditions while I'm there. What should I do?
4. I don't want to move to Los Angeles unless I know I have an audition. Can you get me one?
5. Can you please get me an agent?

The people asking these questions have no idea how casting works, or how agents and casting directors operate. True, before you can become a movie star, you're going to have to audition for a casting director and get a talent agent. Before you can get discovered, you need to know how this happens. Understanding how the casting process works is critical to your success as an actor.

Major movies, TV shows, commercials, plays, and student films are cast in different ways. By looking at each process, you'll learn what the producers, agents, and casting directors do. I'm not going to explain each step of each process in great detail here. That will come later. For now I just want to explain how auditions happen so that you'll know how to get to them.

A production needs to be cast

A writer has written something and now it needs to be produced. This could be an ad for a local furniture store or a movie for Universal Studios starring Meg Ryan. It could even be a local filmmaker who's shooting a video on weekends. We'll just call it a "production." Numerous entities could do this, and it can be done in many ways. That's not your concern. What concerns you is that somebody has written a script and now she needs to find actors.

It all starts with a producer

The producer is the person who runs the whole show. He'll get the money for the production and hire all the people necessary to complete the project. He's the head honcho. He might have purchased a script from a writer or maybe he wrote the script himself. As a producer he now has to hire and supervise all the people necessary to get the production made. One of the most prolific and powerful producers working today is Brian Grazer. He won the 2002 Academy Award for *A Beautiful Mind.* He has also produced *Apollo 13, How the Grinch Stole Christmas, The Cat in the Hat, 8 Mile,* and *Liar Liar.* And TV shows like 24 and *Felicity.*

Even though the producer is ultimately responsible for everything, he doesn't really "do" anything other than make phone calls. He hires all the people who actually make the movie, and he has to guide them all. When a movie wins the Best Picture Academy Award, it's the producer who accepts the trophy because he's the one who put it all together.

Two of the most important hires that a producer will make are the director and the casting director. The director is the person who actually works with the actors and determines the camera movements during the shoot. Directors are responsible for guiding the actors, and they control how the movie looks. Casting directors are in charge of auditioning and casting the actors.

If you decide to make a movie yourself and you find a script, hire a camera operator, and cast your friends to act in it, then you've just done the job of a producer and a casting director. If a furniture store needs a TV commercial shot in Alabama, its management contacts a local production company and hires a producer to make the commercial. Most plays at small theaters have a resident producer who picks scripts and hires directors to perform plays at the theater.

The role of the casting director

A casting director, also called a "CD," is an independent person who actually finds the talent for the production. These are the people who come looking for actors like you. They can find you in lots of ways, but the best way is for your photo and résumé to appear on their desk. That doesn't happen by magic. It starts happening when you get to steps four, five, and six of Your Acting Plan.

If Brian Grazer is producing *The Nutty Professor III,* he'll hire a professional casting director in Los Angeles or New York, depending on where the film is being shot. Casting directors can work multiple projects at one time, and they're always very busy. The producer will give the casting director a script and a list of all the characters and descriptions. It's his or her job to find all the actors.

Most TV shows are cast and shot in Los Angeles. Some are cast and shot in New York. Very few others are shot in other locations like Florida, North Carolina, Vancouver, and Toronto. Casting directors work in the cities where the shows are cast. Therefore, if you want to audition for a TV show like *Friends,* then you have to live in Los Angeles. If you want to audition for *NYPD Blue,* you have to live in New York because that's where it's cast and shot.

If you're auditioning for a play, it's very likely that the director is also doing the casting. If it's a big production at an established theater, there will be a separate casting director. For most smaller theaters, however, the director usually does the casting.

For a local car commercial, the production company will use a local casting director and local actors. If you live in a smaller city, these are the types of casting directors you'll try to contact when you're starting out.

In a very low budget film, like most student productions, the casting director is probably going to be the writer, producer, and maybe even the camera operator, too. As the budget of a project gets smaller, many of the tasks are performed by the same person. When I shot my first film, I was the writer, coproducer, actor, editor, and casting director.

The best way to find out who the casting director or producer is for a TV show or movie is to look through the credits. They get listed along with everyone else. If it goes by too quickly, just do a search for the show on www.imdb. com and you'll see them listed along with all the other production staff. Start a database of entries so that you can keep track of who is out there and what they're casting.

Posting the audition notice

Once the casting director decides what kind of actors she needs, she posts the audition notice. If it's a professionally budgeted production in a major city, it is posted using something called "Breakdown Services." These are also known as "the break-downs." Another service for commercials is called "Commercial Express," but I'm going to call everything "the breakdowns" for now because the idea is the same.

The breakdowns are supplied by Breakdown Services Ltd. They have offices in New York, Los Angeles, and Vancouver. This company receives casting information from casting directors and compiles it all into a list that is sent out to talent agents. The roles listed include television shows, pilots, feature films, movies for television, theater, student films, industrial videos, and Internet projects. The breakdowns aren't made available to the public, and you can't buy them. They are only sent to accredited agents and managers who pay a monthly fee to receive them. That means that you will never hear about any auditions that are sent out through the breakdowns unless you have an agent who receives the breakdowns.

You can, however, visit the company's website, www. breakdownservices.com, and find lots of valuable acting-related information. One great feature of the website is that it lists about half a dozen daily auditions for good things like student films,

"Industrials" are instructional films used by businesses, schools, and product manufacturers. These could include videos like *How to Operate Your New Table Saw,* or *Sexual Harassment in the Workplace.* These types of productions represent a huge opportunity for actors because they're produced in practically every state.

plays, and commercials—three good ways to get exposure. These are legitimate auditions to which anyone can submit.

What I've just discussed answers the first two questions that I presented earlier in this chapter.

1. Can you please tell me how I can audition for *Spiderman 2?*
2. How do I audition for a TV show?

You should now be able to answer these questions. The only way you can audition for *Spiderman 2* or a major TV show is to get an agent who receives the breakdowns. Luckily for you, the steps of Your Acting Plan will teach you how to get such an agent. Second, you have to live in the cities where those agents work. That means Los Angeles or New York. If you don't live in those cities, don't worry about it. It doesn't mean you can't ever be in a movie or TV show. It just means that you have to pursue the opportunities that are available in your area right now.

The local car commercial in Lincoln, Nebraska, is not going to submit audition information through the breakdowns because nobody in Nebraska is subscribing to the breakdowns. Instead, they'll submit their casting needs to the local casting directors who handle those regions. Because there aren't that many productions, these areas have only a few casting companies. That's another reason why it's important to learn who the local casting directors are in your area. You'll learn how to do that in step five.

For most small theaters and low-budget films, the audition notices will be posted on bulletin boards, in the classified section of the local arts publication, and on the Internet. The notices won't be sent to agents because these roles pay little or no money and therefore agents aren't going to get involved. Because these smaller productions are where you're going to start, these are the sources you'll be searching through for most of your first roles.

It's not uncommon to begin working for free, and many actors work free jobs for years. To get that first role, you have to be willing to take what you can get, and that usually means working for free. The "pay" you're getting is in the form of experience. The experience will make you a better actor and will help you in future auditions and productions. The credit you'll receive will expand your résumé. That combination will help get jobs that pay money.

Agents and managers receive the casting notices

Talent agents and some managers receive the breakdowns each morning and start looking at everything that's being cast. Casting happens very quickly. Commercials often need to be cast within a few days. TV shows looking for guest roles need to be cast every week. Movies might take a little longer, but the point

SCAM WARNING!

Roles for major movies and TV shows that go out through the breakdowns are not published on the Internet. Therefore, if you ever see a website that says something like, "Get the latest auditions for TV shows and movies," realize that you're being misled. Do not fall for these. You'll end up paying for useless information.

is that agents receive casting notices through the breakdowns every day. That means new auditions take place every day.

Agents in smaller markets like Portland and Dallas aren't going to have as many roles to fill. It's unlikely that they'll be getting the breakdowns, so they certainly aren't going to be filling roles for major movies or TV shows on a regular basis. They will be working with casting directors on local film shoots, commercials, industrials, and plays. They'll receive notices for whatever is being cast in that area, and that's why it's so important to start with a local agent.

If you don't have an agent or a manager, nobody is going to send you audition notices. Instead, you'll have to find them on your own. Typically you're going to search for the types of smaller auditions that are available to beginners. These will include plays, student films, and other opportunities that are all explained in step four of Your Acting Plan. You'll use these to build a résumé that will allow you to get an agent and get access to better roles.

Headshots and résumés are submitted

Once the agents receive the casting notices, they'll go through the photos and résumés of their actors who fit the appropriate categories and messenger them over to the casting directors. These are actual hard copies of headshots and résumés. The actors' headshots have their résumés stapled to the backs of them. They do not get e-mailed or faxed. Casting directors want to hold the headshots in their hands and look at them.

If you're submitting your own headshots and résumés, you're going to do it the same way that an agent does. You'll put your headshot and résumé in a large envelope and mail it to the casting director along with a brief cover letter. Details for doing that are covered in steps four and five of Your Acting Plan.

The submissions arrive at the casting director's office

Once an audition notice is sent out, casting directors begin receiving hundreds of photos and résumés. They look at the photo first. If they see something they like, they'll turn it over and read the résumé. If they like that, too, they just might give you a call. In most cases they will throw your photo away. Most actors spend years mailing out hundreds or thousands of headshots waiting to get that first good audition. It's a process that takes time.

If this is a smaller production like a student film, then your photo and headshot might land in the living room or dorm room of the student who's making the film. He'll go through the photos with the same scrutiny as a professional casting director. He'll be more forgiving though, because he has a very low budget and he might not be paying you anything at all. Experience and photo quality won't be as important, but even in this situation, there will still be competition. The point is that you always want to communicate the most professional and competent image possible no matter what your level is.

If you're submitting yourself for a play, chances are that you'll just show up for an open audition and hand your headshot to the director on the same day as your audition. In this case the headshot isn't as important, and it might not be necessary at all. But it will still play a part in how others perceive you.

By now you should have the answer to question #3, "I'm making a trip to Los Angeles for two weeks and I'd like to go to some auditions while I'm there. What should I do?" If that's the case, then I would recommend going to Disneyland because you can't establish a residence, get training, secure your contact information, find an agent, submit yourself for auditions, and then wait to get called all in two weeks. You can't really do anything of value in two weeks, so if that's all the time you have, just spend

SCAM WARNING!

Walk into a casting director's office and you might see six people or more on the phones as they open envelopes and look through headshots. You won't see them surfing the Net looking for actors on websites. You won't see them looking through CDs of actors. Therefore, be very careful about websites that say, "Casting directors will find you in our database." These can be very misleading claims.

it at the beach or amusement parks. Becoming an actor requires years of commitment.

Audition notices are sent

After reviewing all the photos and résumés, the casting director picks out the actors she wants to audition. She calls your agent and says, "Hey, Susan, I'd like to see your client for that shoe commercial at noon tomorrow." Your agent or manager then calls you and gives you all the details about the audition.

If you don't have an agent or a manager, the casting director is going to call you directly. When she does, make sure you get the following information. You need to know

- The time of the audition.
- Where it's located.
- If you need to wear anything specific.
- How you can get the sides (a portion of the script).

In Los Angeles especially, casting directors can get very specific about where to go and where to park. Sometimes they might want you to bring a bathing suit, a tool belt, a ball cap, or something else specific to the role.

Sides is an industry term for a portion of the script. It could be one to twenty pages in length. Typically it will be five pages or less. This is just a section of the script that they want you to read. They might fax it to you and they might ask you to come pick it up at the office. They might ask you to use an online service to retrieve it. Websites like www.showfax.com provide sides for a fee. It's an inexpensive service in which you'll pay a fee and download the sides for your project. It's also possible that no sides are available or the sides will be provided when you show up for the audition.

This part of the process doesn't depend on the budget. Whether it's a $10 million budget or a $100 budget, you'll still get a call from someone asking you to come audition. You need to ask the same questions, but don't waste anyone's time with idle chitchat. As mentioned, find out where the audition is, when it is, if you should wear anything in particular, and how you can get the sides. Thank them and hang up. Then mentally prepare yourself for the audition.

The actual audition

Once you get to the audition, anything could happen. You might read a script. You might improv. You might perform a monologue. You might sing. You might jump around the stage like a monkey. You never know what a CD will ask you to do. That's why good training is so important. If you took a beginning acting class four years ago, you might not be prepared. If you've been going to a regular workshop every week where you prac-

A great way to practice script reading is to go to www.showfax.com and download a sample script and practice performing it. Showfax has actual scripts that people are auditioning for right now.

tice improvs, cold readings, and scene study, then you'll probably be much better prepared.

Whatever it is you do, one thing is certain: It will happen very quickly, and then they'll say "thank you, good-bye." That's it.

Anything other than "You're hired" means no

After the CD has seen everyone audition, she might meet with the producer and the director and the client to discuss who should get the part. You might be called back to audition again or you might simply get the part. If you don't get the part, you'll hear nothing. There's no standard wait time, but you usually won't have to wait more than a few days if it's good news. Sometimes they'll call back the same day. I've gone to auditions where all of us auditioned, then we waited in the hallway and the winner was called back in immediately.

If you get the part, casting directors will tell you that you're hired. Anything other than that means you didn't get the part. They won't ask you to call them. They won't tell you to send a thank-you card and follow up in a week. If they want you, they'll let you know. If they don't want you, they'll usually say nothing.

The value of an experienced agent

Now that you see how agents and casting directors interact in the casting process, it should become obvious why it's so important to have a good agent. Show business is built on relationships. An agent who's been in business a long time is going to know a lot of people. He's going to hear about auditions that other agents might not hear about. He's going to talk to producers and directors about projects that nobody else knows about yet. The better connected an agent or a manager is, the more chances he has to find work for his client. That's why you always need to look for a better agent.

> It's possible to get seen by me without an agent or manager, but it is hard to build a career without an agent or manager who knows what's being cast, who has access based on relationships that they've built over a number of years.
>
> —Mark Teschner,
> casting director for *General Hospital*

A word about pilot season

Pilots are proposed TV shows that are made in the winter with the hope that they will become new TV series. The pilot season runs from February to April. During that time, there might be two hundred to three hundred new shows being cast and produced. That means that casting directors will audition lots of actors to fill those roles. Very few of these pilots will become actual TV shows, but some of them will make it.

If you want to get cast in a pilot, then you have to follow the steps of Your Acting Plan. That is, there's nothing special you can do to get cast in a pilot. The roles for the pilots will go out through the breakdowns and agents will submit their actors for auditions. It's a common mistake to think that a new actor can arrive in Los Angeles in January and start getting auditions for pilots. If you want to get cast in a pilot, then you need to get to California and start studying regularly and networking your way toward getting an agent.

Now that you understand the casting process and how the agents and casting directors interact, it's time to learn what they're looking for in an actor and how you can best prepare yourself for success.

Agents and casting directors need someone who lives near them

As you've now learned, casting happens very quickly. That means that the actor has to live in that town and has to be available immediately. You can't get an agent in Los Angeles if you live in Omaha or London. Agents only work with actors who live in their towns.

Agents understand as well as anyone how much commitment and determination is required. If you don't live in New York or Los Angeles, then an agent isn't going to think that you're very serious about acting. Think about it. If you want to act in TV, why live anyplace else but Los Angeles? If you want to perform on Broadway, why would you live anyplace but New York? This doesn't mean that you have to live in these cities when you're starting out. If you live in Dallas, then you need to approach Dallas agents and Dallas casting directors to look for work in Dallas. When you're ready to work in Los Angeles or New York, then you can move to those cities and start contacting agents.

Now you should have the answer to question #4, "I don't want to move to Los Angeles unless I know I have an audition. Can you get me one?"

Keep in mind what I said about your daily goals. If you live in Dallas and you want an agent in Los Angeles, then your daily goal is to move to Los Angeles. Once you get there, then your daily goal can become getting an agent in Los Angeles. If you try to skip that step, then you're likely to stall.

They need actors who know how to act

This doesn't mean that you have to be a graduate of the Yale University Drama Department, but you need to know how to audition and how to act. You can learn it very quickly if you get into a good workshop. Performers like Will Smith, who never had any formal training at all, can learn the craft on their own. You can't go into an audition and not know what a script looks like or how to read one. That's why agents want to see *some* training on your résumé.

If an agent sends an actor to an audition and the actor is terrible, then the CD is not going to think very highly of that agent. Imagine the CD calls an agent and says, "Hey, Sharon, that actor you sent over was horrible. Why are you working with him?" The agent replies, "Oh, really, well, gee, he just moved here from Houston and he said he always wanted to be in the movies and that he'd work real hard." Agents can't afford to take risks on actors who don't know what they're doing. Regardless of the size of the budget, if you want to compete, you have to be good.

They need someone who has a professional headshot and a résumé

When you're auditioning for your first theater role or student film, the quality of your headshot isn't that important, but as you look for better roles and move to bigger markets, it becomes very important. There's no perfect headshot and there are lots of different types, but if it's of poor quality, then you're seriously hurting your credibility.

When you get to the Los Angeles and New York markets, the headshot is extremely important, and nothing less than a completely professional job is acceptable. Agents receive headshots every day from actors like you who want agents. If you have some crummy scanned photo of your high school graduation, and a poorly formatted résumé on fancy paper, then you can't be taken seriously. No real agent is going to call you if you can't present yourself professionally, because you're already making his life difficult.

Casting directors are going to judge you the same way. If your headshot and résumé are bad, they are going to look at that as inexperience and lacking in dedication. They'll toss you in favor of someone who has his act together.

I don't want you to panic now and think you have to spend hundreds of dollars on headshots. Step three of Your Acting Plan is going to explain exactly what you need, what it should look like, and how to get it. Notice that the headshot is step three, not step one or two. I'll explain what you need to do once you're ready for it. For now, just keep in mind that you'll have to get one eventually, and you should try to get the best quality possible.

They need someone who can be reached

As I mentioned earlier, auditions can happen anytime, and they could be anyplace in an agent's area. Therefore, an agent must be able to contact you immediately. If you work in a warehouse, you'll need a pager or cell phone or you'll have to call your message machine every hour. If an agent can't get in touch with you in a couple of hours, she might not be able to get you to an audition. That's a potential job you could lose.

When you're starting out and you're auditioning for low-budget productions, you might have auditions on the weekend. I once turned on my cell phone on a Monday morning only to hear the following message: "Hi Pete, I just got your headshot. I know it's last minute, but we're having auditions today, Sunday, between one and four. Call me and I'll give you directions." I missed out. You need to be reachable.

They need someone who can speak in standard American English

Standard American English is the way the network news anchors and talk-show hosts speak. People like Peter Jennings,

Matt Lauer, Diane Sawyer, Katie Couric, David Letterman, and Jay Leno all speak in standard American English. They don't have any discernible regional accent.

Watch any American television show, commercial, or movie and count the number of people who speak with foreign accents. You'll only need a few fingers to do this because you won't hear many. That includes regional dialects like American Southern and New York. I'm not saying it's right, wrong, good, or bad. That's just the way it is. If you want to be an actor, you need to learn how to speak in standard American English before you even think of meeting with an agent or casting director. After you get the part, you can speak to them with your natural accent and show them how good you are, but until then, don't let them know that you have an accent.

If you're a well-known actor in your native country or if you have some other quality that makes you bankable, then this rule doesn't apply. For example, Arnold Schwarzenegger has a very strong accent, but Arnold broke into the movies utilizing his skills as a bodybuilder and bigger-than-life persona. In short, he brought name recognition with him and plenty of charisma. If you don't have that, then an accent is going to hinder you.

If you have an accent, it doesn't mean you can't make it. It just means that you're adding another obstacle to an already difficult task.

Agents need someone who doesn't look exactly like one of their clients

A manager once showed me a headshot and cover letter from an actor who he said was perfect. The letter was short, smart, and friendly. The headshot was professional. The actor was young and pretty, and her résumé showed some solid beginner credits.

The manager said that this was exactly what he looks for in new talent. I asked him what he would do next with that actor. He said, "Nothing. I already have a girl of this type whom I represent." This girl actually missed out because she looked like a typical attractive TV star.

By now you should have enough information to answer question #5, "Can you get me an agent?" Only *you* can get yourself an agent. Even if I did wield the power to get agents for people, how could I recommend you when I don't know anything about your look, your training, where you live, your experience, or whether you can speak English?

ACTION POINTS

- You have to learn about the casting process so that you understand how agents and casting directors work and what they're looking for.
- You need to find out what kinds of roles you can submit yourself for and what kinds of roles require an agent.
- You need to approach the agents and opportunities in your area.

DAILY GOALS

I want you to do a performance for somebody. Here's your scene. I want you to describe the entire casting process to somebody. To do this, you'll have to study this chapter and learn the process inside and out. Once you know the process well enough to explain it to somebody else, you will have educated yourself in a way that will protect you from getting scammed by people who will try to sell you bogus shortcuts.

Go ahead and actually tell someone how an actor gets cast. Describe the role of the casting director, the producer, the agent, and the actor. If you can't do this, then it means that you don't understand the process. If you don't understand the process, then your career might stall because you don't know what to do next.

This daily goal should not be a chore. It should be a fun performance for you. Get dramatic with it if you wish. It's a great way to answer the question "What did you do today to advance your acting career?"

3

YOUR ACTING PLAN

The most intelligent man living cannot succeed in accumulating money—nor in any other undertaking—without plans which are practical and workable.

Napoleon Hill, *Think and Grow Rich*

Now that you understand how the casting process works, you'll have a better idea about what your goals are and how you can formulate a plan to achieve them. I'll be referring back to chapter 2 on occasion because it contains most of the reasons you're doing all these steps. As long as you keep trying, you'll have a shot at success. Having said that, I should add that it's very important to have some kind of plan.

Just about all actors I've ever met tell a similar story about how they got started in Hollywood. They usually say that they got to town and just kind of figured it out over the course of a few years. They tried this, then they tried that. Many got scammed. They got involved with a bad manager or they got the wrong photos. Then they quit. Then they started again. They figured it out eventually, but by that time, they had wasted a lot of time and money and they weren't as young as they used to be. They also usually add that if they'd known then what they know now, it would've been a lot easier and faster.

What's even more disconcerting is that even if you know what you're doing, it takes time to succeed. Brad Pitt didn't just move to Hollywood and become a star the first year. If you're talented, hardworking, and dedicated, it can still take years to find real success. That's why you need to get organized immediately and start your systematic approach.

Seven steps

Here are the seven steps you're going to follow. First I'll list them, and then I'll briefly explain what's involved with each one. These are explained clearly in subsequent chapters, but I want you to look at them now so you can see what you'll be doing. Later I'll ask you to write these down and take notes. Keep in mind that success can come at any point, but it won't come if you don't do something about it.

1. Take the acting tests.
2. Learn how to act.
3. Acquire the basics: headshot, résumé, business card, post-cards, demo reel, contact info, monologue, job.
4. Find auditions on your own.
5. Contact agents and casting directors.
6. Work with agents and managers on your career.
7. Always be networking.

1. TAKE THE ACTING TESTS

Whenever people ask me if I think they can become an actor, I ask them to sing a song out loud right there, no matter where we are. If they sing the song, I tell them they have a pretty good chance. If they don't or won't, then I tell them that they don't have much of a chance. The reason is because making it as an actor requires more courage and passion than most people realize.

The biggest misconception about acting is that it's all about looks and "talent." Those things can help, but they aren't nearly as important as courage and desire. Winning an Academy Award is all about your technical abilities as a professional actor. However, breaking into the business is all about your desire and determination. If you want to find out if you have what it takes, don't try to measure your ability to learn lines or sing. Instead, try to measure your ability to take risks and never give up. That's what the acting tests will do. These simple tests measure just that, and if you can pass them, you just might have what it takes.

2. LEARN HOW TO ACT

If you want to be an actor, one of the first things you have to do is learn how to act. You might think that I'm talking about universities or acting academies. Those might help, but they're just two of the many options. Learning to act might not require any schooling at all. Plenty of famous actors have achieved success without any type of training, but they still had to learn how to act.

Learning to act might involve a local workshop or university, or it might be as simple as reading a play out loud in your bedroom. This does not necessarily mean that you need a coach or a teacher or that you have to acquire a technique. Learning to act means finding a way to prepare yourself so that you're ready to walk into a room of strangers and give a great audition. There isn't any one way to do that, and I'll help you find the best way for you.

3. ACQUIRE THE BASICS: HEADSHOT, RÉSUMÉ, BUSINESS CARDS, POSTCARDS, DEMO REEL, CONTACT INFO, MONOLOGUE, JOB

Essentially these are all the things that you'll need to have when you actually begin searching for work. You don't need them all at once, and they don't have to cost a fortune. I cover these in the beginning because they're commonly used items that you should be aware of, and they're also a source of great controversy and debate.

There are many opinions about what a headshot should look like and how to format a résumé. I want you to be aware of the basic essentials, but more important, I don't want you to think that any of these will make or break your career. What's most important is to keep busy and to keep trying. I don't want you to get bogged down worrying about a headshot. I'll give you enough information so that you'll be able to get a decent headshot, résumé, and monologue, and I'll cover all those other terms so that you'll know how and when they're used. This alone will save you a lot of time and money.

4. FIND AUDITIONS ON YOUR OWN

This is one of the most exciting steps because you'll learn just how many opportunities are out there for beginners to break into the business. I list specific sources for finding acting roles that will help you build experience and add credits to your résumé. Many books talk about agent interviews and contracts, but I'll show you how to actually find acting roles. It doesn't matter where you live, something is always available, and that's the way you have to think.

Too many beginners make the mistake of trying to get their first role in a Steven Spielberg film. That's not likely to happen. It's all a building process. From backyard plays to national commercials, I'll teach you how to find what's available in your area, and I'll teach you how to keep trying and building experience.

5. CONTACT AGENTS AND CASTING DIRECTORS

When you think you're ready to contact agents and casting directors, I'll give you detailed instructions on exactly how to do it. I'll supply you with sample cover letters along with a list of resources for locating the people in your area who can help you. I'll introduce a systematic process for finding agents, contacting them, and following up. You'll know exactly how and where to find them.

The unique feature of this lesson is that I explain how your experience and geographic location affect this step. If you live in Alabama, you're going to approach this much differently from someone who lives in Los Angeles. You have to understand the process in order to do this. Agents are not going to come looking for you. You have to go looking for them. If you know how to do this, you'll increase your chances dramatically.

6. WORK WITH AGENTS AND
MANAGERS ON YOUR CAREER

Many actors think that once they've landed an agent or a manager, they're home free and they don't have to do much anymore. Nothing could be further from the truth. Landing an agent or a manager is only half the battle, and most actors are forced to work even harder at that point. Because they don't know much, actors are often confused and frustrated when the agent they worked so hard to get doesn't appear to do anything. That's why it's very important to know what's expected of you once you get to this point.

Getting an agent or a manager is not your main goal. Your main goal is to get auditions. A good agent or manager can help you get better auditions than you can get on your own, but you still have to work. Therefore, it's important to realize that working with agents and managers is just another stop on your road to success. I'll give you specific recommendations about what to say to your agent and how to establish your relationship so that you'll know exactly what's going on and exactly what's expected of you.

7. ALWAYS BE NETWORKING

Networking is not something extra that you do if you have the time and want to meet people, and it's more than just going to parties. Networking is the single most important aspect of getting discovered and I'll explain why. It's almost impossible to get ahead in show business without talking to people, meeting strangers, seeking advice, and making contacts. That's what networking is all about. This is an industry built entirely on relationships. Knowing this will give you a huge advantage and will help you move toward your goal much quicker. A successful actor never stops networking.

Networking doesn't imply that you'll be at cocktail parties making small talk with Hollywood producers, although that might happen. Networking involves being aware of who you need to meet and how to meet them. It involves seeking out people and resources that can help you reach your goals no matter where you live.

The steps never end

Even though I've only listed seven steps, I don't want you to think that you can complete them quickly and then you're done and you're a successful actor. That is not going to happen. The steps of this plan have to be worked constantly and continuously. This is called "working the cycle." It means that you're going to study, get photos, look for an agent and auditions. Then you're going to study and look for auditions and maybe get a new headshot and look for a better agent. If you become a successful actor, you'll find that this process never ends.

Once you understand all the steps of the plan, you'll always have something to do and you'll be able to set daily goals for yourself that are attainable and that will bring you closer to your overall goal. When you actually get an agent or an audition, it won't be because of some huge stroke of luck, like winning the lottery. Instead, it will just be another step of the plan.

Remember that becoming a star or becoming famous is not a step. You can't just *do* that. However, getting a photo is a step that you can do. All the steps of Your Acting Plan are things that you can actually do. If you do them consistently and don't give up, it's possible that you just might become a star or become famous.

Success can happen at any time

It's possible that you could get cast in a TV commercial at your very first audition. It's also possible that you'll toil for fifteen years before you get a break. The idea is that you stay on one step until you complete it. You might come back to it later as you're working the cycle, but you need to avoid skipping around and just trying various steps in a random fashion.

You might bounce back and forth between steps one and two for a few years. You might bounce back and forth between one and four. Some actors with whom I've worked have gone from zero acting experience to signing with an agent in two months. Some actors go to classes for years before they even get their first headshot taken, because they lack the confidence and skills to go on auditions. You'll discover that the steps aren't always as clear as they might seem.

Each step builds and leads to the next one. Actors who skip to step five usually fail and get impatient and then quit. Then they tell other aspiring actors how impossible it is to make it. Follow the steps in order no matter how easy or difficult they are. Remember that most actors don't fail; most actors quit.

The supplies you'll need

I'll be asking you to accumulate some things along the way, and I promise that these won't be terribly expensive. If you're serious about becoming an actor, then you'll be able to spend a few dollars to organize yourself and put yourself in the best position to succeed.

You'll need two types of calendars. I recommend a large wall calendar. I like the dry erasable kind with large squares for each day. I hang mine right next to my desk where I can look at it daily. You'll also need an appointment book or PDA that's small enough to carry with you to auditions and other meetings. Get in the habit of looking at that book each day. You'll become much more organized and efficient. You can use a calendar system in your computer if you have a good one. Yahoo! and many other websites provide free online calendars that e-mail your daily tasks to you. I like those and use them for some things, but I still prefer the wall calendar because I can always look at it without having to turn it on.

I also recommend that you get some kind of notebook. A simple three-ring binder with dividers and paper can still be found for a few dollars at a local office supply store.

The calendar is going to be your daily guide. Try to put a task on it every day or every week. For every night this week you can simply write, "Read *Act Now!*" At the end of each day, when you ask yourself what you did to advance your acting career, you'll be able to say that you read your book and that will be enough. Later, you'll be putting other tasks on there.

The appointment book is what you'll carry with you daily. You'll need to start keeping track of names, phone numbers, e-mail addresses, and appointments. Carry it with you from now on and make a point of looking at it each day along with your wall calendar. You're going to start putting entries in there and you'll need to be organized. The notebook is going to fill up as you network, but I'll address that more specifically later. The important thing is that you give yourself a daily task to accomplish. The more frequently you accomplish these tasks, the faster you'll reach your goal. It's that simple.

Treat your acting like any business

Before I began writing this book, a good friend of mine had recently lost her job. After taking the weekend off, she got up at 7:00 A.M., ate breakfast, and got dressed in her business clothes. I said, "What are you doing? You don't have a job anymore." She said that in order to find another job, she had to treat her job search like she would any other business. She wouldn't take any days off except on the weekend. My friend "worked" each day from eight to five looking for a job. She made calls, looked through the paper, sent résumés, and wrote letters. It was during a time of severe unemployment, and she found a new job in just six weeks.

My friend probably wasn't smarter or more qualified than most of the thousands of people who were also out of work. The difference was in her work ethic and determination. As I saw her "working," I had no doubt that she would find a new job very quickly. That is how you have to treat your search for a career in acting—like a job.

You need to decide how much time you can dedicate to acting, and you need to stick to your schedule. You might start with Wednesday nights or Saturday mornings. Maybe, if you're in school, you spend two hours daily after school rehearsing a play. If you're a bartender, then you can spend each day between 10 A.M. and noon working on your letters, and networking and reading and rehearsing. Whatever time you decide to devote to acting, stick to it and try to increase it. If you decrease it, you'll probably end up giving up. And don't just cancel your acting time, either. It should be the last thing you ever give up, not the first. The better you are at sticking to your schedule, the better off you'll be.

Why don't I just get a manager and let him do all this?

Many actors are tempted to go hire a manager as the first step of their career. That's not a terrible idea, but it's just not wise to do that until you've educated yourself better. Some industry professionals advise against getting managers until you actually have something to manage. Some would say that in today's market, actors have to have a manager in order to succeed. There's truth in both of these statements and I think it's a matter of timing.

When you're brand-new to acting, who's going to manage you? You have no experience and you don't know much. How valuable could you possibly be? The types of managers who want to work with people like you are usually scam artists or just ineffective managers hoping to get lucky with a new prospect. If you go looking for a manager as your first step, you're likely to get conned or heartbroken or both. I can't count the number of e-mails I get from beginners who say, "Pete, I found this great manager, but he wants to charge me a lot of money to get started and to . . ." Whoa, hold on! Back up! He wants to *charge* you a fee? This is just one of the reasons you don't want to hire a manager right away.

Another reason not to hire a manager right away is because you don't need one right away. As you'll soon learn in the plan, you're going to spend your first months or years practicing in some kind of class. You'll also be looking for mostly low-paying or nonpaying jobs because these are the roles that are open to beginners. You'll be building experience and knowledge as you look for an agent. That doesn't mean you can't get discovered or hit something big in your first month; it's just not likely to happen. A good manager wants an actor who is trained, organized, and motivated and knows something about the business. It's going to take you a while before you fit that profile. Think of your first year as an educational period.

How do I find the time?

Lazy people always complain that they don't have enough time. There are twenty-four hours in a day. If you can't find time for acting, then you simply don't want to be an actor. There is always time to do the things we're passionate about.

Don't use sleep as an excuse, either. It's common knowledge that the laziest, least energetic people are the ones who sleep the most. The most intelligent, creative, dynamic, and energetic person I ever met only sleeps two hours a day. That's not a lie, and that doesn't involve doing drugs. There are yogis in India who can stay awake for a month at a time. You only need as much sleep as you think you need. Don't let parents, doctors, friends, or even me tell you how much sleep you need. Whatever your mind tells you that you need is what you need. If you want some examples, read the book *Autobiography of a Yogi* and you'll learn amazing things about the potential of the human mind and spirit.

ACTION POINTS

- Stick to a clearly defined plan.
- Treat your pursuit of acting like a business.
- Schedule a regular amount of time to act.

DAILY GOALS

Gather your supplies and write down the steps of Your Acting Plan on page one of your notebook. It's very important to look at those steps each day. On pages two through eight in your notebook, I want you to write the name of each step at the top of the page. Therefore, the top of page two says, "Take the Acting Tests." The top of page three says, "Learn How to Act." You're going to fill each of these sheets with notes and tips that you'll learn as you read about the various steps.

This is one of the easiest assignments you'll have, but you should be excited because you now have a clearly defined plan and you're finally working your way toward becoming an actor. Once you've organized your supplies, you will have answered the question "What did you do today to advance your acting career?"

4

STEP ONE OF YOUR ACTING PLAN: TAKE THE ACTING TESTS

AFTER reading the outline of Your Acting Plan, you now realize that you need to set up a schedule and budget some time toward your pursuit of acting. You have some kind of calendar to schedule your activities, and you understand that the most important element is your desire to stick to the plan. Now that you have that, you're going to start the first step of the plan.

How do you know if you have what it takes to be an actor? Is it your look? Is it your voice or your dancing ability? What is it? If it was *just* about talent, then every talented person would be acting. I have plenty of friends who are wildly talented actors, comedians, and singers, yet they aren't in show business. That's because it takes a lot more than just natural talent. Many aspiring actors never get past the aspiring part because they simply lack the courage and desire necessary to succeed. Others start but quit because they aren't determined enough.

Nearly every actor who ever made it can tell you all the stories about the crummy jobs, the times they almost gave up, the self-doubt, and the depression. They'll finish their story by saying something like, "But I just couldn't give up. I had to go on one more audition." That's what it's all about.

> History has demonstrated that the most notable winners usually encountered heartbreaking obstacles before they triumphed. They won because they refused to become discouraged by their defeats.
>
> —B. C. Forbes

Courage and desire

> You know what's even more important than talent? Desire.
> —Patricia Heaton,
> star of *Everybody Loves Raymond*

I use the terms *courage* and *desire* because they are the two most important things you need to be a successful actor. I'm always getting e-mails from actors who want to know if they have what it takes to make it. What they should really be asking is do they have what it takes to get started. It would be easier to succeed if the first step was to shoot a scene in a big movie with a star like Al Pacino, but that's not the first step. Even if you're a brilliantly talented actor, getting to the point where you have a good agent who gets you good auditions could take years of hard work, courage, and determination. So whenever someone asks me if they have what it takes, what they're really saying is *Do you think I have enough courage and desire to break into acting?*

Without knowing a person, I have no way of knowing if he or she has these qualities, and that's why I devised these tests—so that you can discover for yourself whether you have what it takes. They won't cost you any money and you won't have to move. Start taking these tests today and keep doing them until you pass. You can do them all in one week if you want or you can do one a month. It might take you two years before you have the courage to do them all, and that's okay. As soon as you're able to do these, you will have proven to yourself that you have the courage and determination necessary to become an actor. Even if you never make it as an actor, these tests will help you become a more outgoing, interesting, and creative person. Once you've read them, I'll explain how I used these elements to get my SAG card and to get a role in *The Mask* with Jim Carrey.

> Courage is rarely reckless or foolish . . . courage usually involves a highly realistic estimate of the odds that must be faced.
>
> —Margaret Truman,
> daughter of President Harry Truman

The Acting Tests

TEST 1(A)

Walk over to your neighbor's house and ask to borrow a pair of socks. Why you need them is up to you. Try not to spend any time thinking about your story. Just walk over and ask for a pair of socks. If he asks you why, you'll have to improvise a reason. If he won't give them to you, that's okay. The important thing is to try.

What this will test This is going to test your courage because, as you've probably surmised, it's not normal to do this sort of thing, and we are very afraid of doing things that aren't normal. I know you want to go on auditions, but do you have any idea what they're really like? Here's a typical audition.

You show up at a studio or rehearsal space and wait with twenty other actors. You'll sign in and you'll sit and study your lines. Maybe there aren't any lines and you'll just wait and wonder. You'll look around at all the other actors and you'll start judging yourself. You'll wonder if you're tall enough or short enough. You'll wonder if you wore the right clothes or if you're as good-looking as that other actor. You'll grow nervous. Then you'll get called into a room.

When you enter the room, there might be one or five people seated facing the stage and they won't say much. You'll then stand before them and perform with very little instruction or direction. Then it's over. It was so fast and you weren't even ready. You weren't relaxed. You didn't know what to say. That's because you were scared to death. That's a normal reaction. Everyone goes through that. How will you handle it? Trust me when I say that if you can walk up to your neighbor and find a creative way to ask him for a pair of socks, you definitely have the courage and creativity to survive an audition. If, however, you're too scared or you're not able to think without a script, then forget about becoming an actor just yet because it's a lot harder than just walking up to your neighbor and asking for a pair of socks.

TEST 1(B)

Set your alarm clock to get up an hour earlier than you normally do. If you usually get up at eight, set your alarm for seven. When it goes off, immediately get up and start your day. Do not hit the snooze button and do not go back to sleep. Do this for one week straight.

What this will test This is going to seriously test your determination. When you reach for the snooze button, say this, "I'd rather sleep than be an actor." I'm not saying that you have to get up early in the morning to be an actor. All I'm doing is testing your determination by giving you an obstacle that you have to overcome.

Patricia Heaton spent years struggling in New York with no money. She lived in crappy apartments and worked crappy jobs, and she got so depressed that she contemplated suicide. Yet something inside of her would not let her give up, and she found the determination to move to Los Angeles and continue her pursuit of acting. Even though she's a talented actress, nobody would ever have known that if she hadn't first displayed the determination necessary to finally get that TV audition.

You need to find out if you have that same kind of determination, but maybe you're not ready or able to move to New York yet and struggle for ten years. Instead, you can try this simple test. If you can't do it, then you're not a very determined person and you just answered the question "Do I have the determination to make it?"

> To map out a course of action and follow it to an end requires some of the same courage that a soldier needs.
>
> —Ralph Waldo Emerson

TEST 2(A)

Next time you're in an elevator with strangers, begin talking and don't stop until the elevator stops.

What this will test You have to realize that absolutely nothing is stopping you from physically doing this. That is, I assume you can speak, and there are no laws against speaking in elevators, although it seems as though there are. So let's look at the thoughts you might possibly have when trying to do this.

1. I'm not going to do that because that's a stupid test. Translation: *I'm afraid to do that.*

2. They might tell me to be quiet or they might think I'm really strange. Translation: *I'm afraid of what people think about me.*
3. It might take five minutes and I wouldn't know what to say. Translation: *I'm afraid that I'm not creative enough to talk for five minutes without a script.*

In other words, the things that prevent you from doing this are that you're afraid to perform, you judge yourself, and you don't have the ability to improvise. Next time you meet an agent or casting director, say this, "Hi, I'd like to be an actor but I'm afraid to perform, I always judge myself, and I can't improvise." Then ask them if they would like to hire you. What do you think they're going to say?

Here's a quote from casting director Annie McCarthy when asked what she looks for in an actor: "Generally, I'm looking for good energy, being open to trying all different things, not being scared of anything. Don't be scared of failing." Annie helped cast *Spy Kids, Cruel Intentions, Scary Movie,* and *Training Day,* so she knows what she's doing.

TEST 2(B)

Try going an entire day without eating. You can drink all the fluids you want, but don't eat.

What this will test I'm not asking you to do this so that you can lose weight. Nobody will change their weight by skipping one day of eating—and no, this isn't dangerous. The human body can go for a month without food if it has to. The reason I'm asking you to do this is to again test your determination.

One of the first actors I mentored got a role in a play that was ninety minutes from where he worked. Each night after his eight-hour work shift, he drove to the theater, rehearsed for two hours, then drove home. Then he got up the next day and did it all over again. That's five hours every night in addition to his eight-hour workday just to do a free play to get a credit on his résumé.

One night he called me and we talked about how tired he was and how hard it was to keep going. I asked him what was harder, the work he was doing for this play or going without food for one day. He laughed and said that going without food for a *week* would be easier than making that three-hour drive each night after work. He landed his first agent shortly thereafter. That's the kind of discipline and dedication it takes.

TEST 3(A)

Sing a song out loud, without music, in front of a person or group of people. It could be something as simple as "Happy Birthday." Try to do it on a public bus or train. If you're in school, stand up in your cafeteria and sing. If you have a "bad" voice, you get extra points.

What this will test Most people who read this book won't do this unless they have a "good" voice. That's because we are afraid of what others think of us. When you're onstage or at an audition, you can't be afraid of what they might think and you can't judge yourself. If you do, your chances of giving an interesting performance are very slim. Casting directors can sense when actors are scared and safe, and they don't pick those kinds of actors.

In all of my acting workshops, I always ask each actor to sing a song. Here's what I have discovered by doing this: Those who refuse to sing never give interesting performances as actors, and they rarely come back to my class. Those who do sing, regardless of how they sound, are far more interesting as actors because they aren't afraid to try anything.

Imagine going to an audition and a casting director asks you to sing a song. Are you going to say, "No, sorry, I'd rather not"? You'll never get another audition from that casting director. Rent a Woody Allen film called *Everyone Says I Love You* and you'll see regular actors singing with regular voices because they are unafraid.

> It takes a lot of courage to show your dreams to someone else.
>
> —Erma Bombeck

TEST 3(B)

Do not watch any television for an entire week.

What this will test This will accomplish two things. You'll really test your determination, and you'll have so much free time that you'll be able to finally focus on your acting. I'm not knocking television. I love television. Currently my favorite shows are *The Sopranos, Scrubs,* and *24.* I mention this test because if you can go a week without watching TV, then you just might have enough determination to keep going when times get tough. This also forces you to do something else with your time.

Do you know that superstar Vin Diesel worked as a telemarketer selling lightbulbs? He was trying to save up money to make his own movie. He called people up and sold them lightbulbs, and he didn't spend his money on fancy cars and a nice apartment. Instead he saved every penny until he had banked $45,000. He used that money to make a film. Steven Spielberg saw the film and cast him in *Saving Private Ryan.* Now he's one of Hollywood's biggest action stars. Do you have that kind of discipline? If you can't go one week without watching TV, then the answer is probably no.

Once you pass the test, though, start watching TV again, because it's important to know what's going on in the entertainment world, and contrary to popular belief, there are some great shows on TV.

TEST 4(A)

Next time you see one of your close friends, tell him or her that you're moving out of town. Go with it as long as you can and really try to convince your friend that you're moving.

What this will test I think this test is one of the most fun. Challenge yourself to convince the other person that you are really moving. Fine acting is not about lying, it's about telling the truth. When you're onstage, you have to speak your lines as though you really mean them. If you do this, then the audience will believe you and they'll say, "Wow, that's a good actor." If you can be so real that you could actually convince a close friend that you're moving, then you just might have what it takes to be a fine performer.

> What would life be if we had no courage to attempt anything?
>
> —Vincent Van Gogh

TEST 4(B)

Sit still in silence for ten minutes. You can sit on a chair or on the edge of your bed, but you can't lie down, talk, or listen to music. Try not to move or think about anything.

What this will test This will accomplish many things. First it will test your determination. If you don't have the determination and willpower to sit still for ten minutes, then forget about becoming an actor, because making it in show business is a lot harder.

The second thing this will teach you is how to relax. Sitting still for ten minutes on a regular basis will force you to relax, and you'll soon find that you can concentrate much more easily, and you can remain calm. Those are the characteristics of fine actors. It's not uncommon for actors, singers, and even professional athletes to spend a few minutes alone in quiet before they go on their respective stages. It's simply a way to focus.

If you actually try to become an actor, you might have to struggle for five years or twenty years before you make it. That requires a lot of patience. If you can't even sit still for ten minutes at a time, then you might want to reconsider your goals.

TEST 5(A)

Walk up to a stranger on the street and say, "Excuse me. I've locked my keys in my car and I need to borrow a quarter to call my roommate (or wife or husband, brother, father . . .)." And don't tell them that you're acting.

What this will test Like some of the other exercises, this will not only test your courage, but it will also test your abilities as an actor. If you don't have the courage, you'll never approach anyone. If you're a lousy actor, you won't collect a dime.

Every beginner at some point has to call a stranger or walk into a stranger's office and convince him that he's a good actor. If you can't even walk up to a stranger and ask for a quarter, how are you going to walk up to an agent and ask her to work for you for free?

TEST 5(B)

Write a thoughtful letter to someone—not an e-mail. Actually write out a letter to someone and mail it. Don't make a joke out of it. You have to mail it to the person.

What this will test Before you land your first agent, you're going to have to write dozens of letters. You're going to send letters to agents, casting directors, and producers. That takes time, dedication, and intelligence. Also, contrary to popular belief, most actors are not empty-headed simpletons. Acting is one of the most creative jobs in the world. If you can't write a simple letter to someone, then you're probably not a very interesting or creative person and therefore you won't have much of a future as an actor.

While doing these tests, don't tell anyone that you're acting. Also, don't hide behind any accents, fake illnesses, or injuries. The best way to do these is simply to approach the subjects with a straight face and speak the truth. Even though you're playing a part, the way to be convincing is to tell the truth in a believable manner.

What do these tests have to do with becoming an actor?

Anybody who lives outside of the big cities will tell you that becoming an actor requires great looks and talent. Even though that's true, if you ever talk to agents, managers, or actors who are actually in the business, they'll tell you that in order to make it, you've got to have a ton of courage and two tons of determination. That's exactly what these tests measure. As you look them over again, you'll notice that the "a" tests measure your courage and the "b" tests measure your determination. Almost all of them test your acting creativity.

> Within each of us is a hidden store of courage. Courage to give us the strength to face any challenge. Within each of

us is a hidden store of determination. Determination to
keep us in the race when all seems lost."

—Roger Dawson, author of
Secrets of Power Negotiating

Remember that the goal as a beginner is to get an agent and to
get auditions. To do that, you're going to have to perform in
front of strangers, and you're also going to have to network with
strangers. That is, you'll have to introduce yourself to people
you've never met. You'll have to cold call. You'll have to hit the
street and knock on doors. How do you know if you'll be able to
do that? It's simple. If you can pass these tests, then you definitely have what it takes to get started.

A dilemma that beginners often face comes during that first
tricky part of their career when they get an acting job that
doesn't pay enough to live on, but the only way they can take
that part is to quit their job. Here's a scenario you might want
to consider. You've exhausted all your vacation at work. You
get cast in a film that's shooting for two weeks in another city.
It only pays expenses, but it's a great role and the director is
going to enter it into a film festival in six months. Your boss is
not going to give you that time off. You'll have to quit. Could
you do that?

Do you have the courage to quit your job right now? If you
become an actor, then you might have to, and you might have to
look for a different job in a month. You might have to quit ten
jobs in your career, and you might not ever make any money as
an actor. If you're too secure in your job, then you're increasing
the already huge odds that you won't make it. There's nothing
wrong with having a safe, secure job, but it's very difficult to
succeed in acting if you're afraid to let it go.

Do you realize that your town has a theater that will be holding auditions for some kind of play soon? If there isn't one in

your town, then there's one in a town that isn't too far away. Physically speaking, nothing is preventing you from going to that theater and asking the manager when the next auditions are. You could walk down to a theater right now and inquire about auditions, yet you don't. Why? Your excuses might include the following: I work at night; I have no experience; they don't take new people; I'm not ready yet; I'm too busy; and so on. Let me translate all of these excuses for you: *I don't have the courage to walk down to that theater and find out about auditions. I'm too inhibited (scared) to walk up to the theater manager and talk to him.*

Even if you find the courage to actually go to a theater, you'll still need to clear a second hurdle. Eventually you'll have to perform in front of somebody. Even though you might have the courage to get up onstage, you'll need even more courage to take risks onstage so that a casting director will look at you and say, "Hmm, that actor is different."

Reducing your inhibitions

> I think you can learn more about acting from psychology books than you can from any acting teacher.
>
> —Tim Robbins

What do you suppose Robbins means? He means that an understanding of inhibition and shyness and how to overcome them are found in psychology books, but they're rarely found in most acting classes. Believe it or not, there was a time when you were very young and you could laugh, sing, make funny faces, and play in the sand, and you didn't care what anybody thought. But then your parents, friends, schools, and everything else taught you to be afraid. They didn't realize it and neither did you, but now you're so inhibited that you won't even sneeze in public for fear of what people might think. Don't worry. You're not alone.

Many famous and gifted actors share the same feelings, but somehow they find the courage to take risks and perform.

> Many of our fears are tissue paper thin, and a single courageous step would carry us through them.
> —Brendan Francis

Psychologist Andrew Salter, in his marvelous book *Conditioned Reflex Therapy,* talks about how our inhibitions are the root of numerous problems, especially in regard to courage, and he suggests ways to overcome shyness through its opposite element: "excitation." In short, he said, "Inhibition is paralysis. Excitation is life." If you're a shy person onstage, you're paralyzed. If you're not shy, then you're alive. This is what you need to understand as an actor. Here's what Salter said about someone with an inhibited personality:

> He must always be prodded. He must always be encouraged. They wait for someone to come to the rescue. They are slow in making decisions because they have nothing to make decisions with. They hesitate and fluctuate. They would not cross the street if their lives depended on it. The inhibitory have developed the brake habit. They have collided with too many automobiles on the highway of life and have learned to drive with the brakes on.

If you're the type of person who "must always be encouraged," then maybe you're not just lazy. Maybe you have some kind of fear that you need to overcome. When it comes to your career, do you "hesitate and fluctuate"? If you're one of those people who has e-mailed my website and asked me to get you an agent, then you need to stop waiting for someone "to come to the rescue."

Having learned this, you now need to overcome this inhibition so that you can move forward as an actor. Salter has an effective solution that will help you do this. He calls it *excitation*. In short, excitation is the opposite of shyness. He suggests six techniques to help you overcome your inhibition so that you can lead a more creative, productive life. The actual techniques listed are his. The explanations are my interpretation of his ideas.

1. **Feeling talk**—This means essentially that you should express opinions, feelings, and thoughts freely with complete disregard for what others think, say, or do. This is not simply reciting facts freely but expressing emotions and not being afraid to give an opinion. Throw away your premeditated utterances and say what you feel when you feel it. A cat purrs when it's content. A dog howls when its paw is stepped on.
2. **Facial talk**—Do not be afraid to use your whole body to express yourself.
3. **Contradict and attack**—Do not peaceably go along with things that you do not agree with.
4. **Deliberate use of the word I**—I like, I want, I heard, and so on. Stop feeling that you must be polite toward everyone and concerned with what everyone else thinks.
5. **Express agreement when you are praised**—Believe the compliments you receive and agree with them wholeheartedly.
6. **Improvisation**—Don't plan. Trust yourself completely that whatever you do and say will be fine.

People who have employed these techniques have experienced dramatic changes in their lives. By reducing their inhibitions, they have become fearless, more creative, and far more assertive. These are the traits of fine actors. Reread the acting tests and you'll see that doing these are ways that you can practice the six techniques Salter recommends for reducing inhibition. They all require that you make a conscious effort to improvise, be assertive, use your face, use the word *I,* and express your feelings. By practicing these tests you can measure your inhibition, and you can reduce it by trying again and again.

Great actors are fearless

Remember that famous scene in *Risky Business* when Tom Cruise danced around in his underwear, singing along with that classic Bob Seger song "Old Time Rock and Roll"? Would you be able to do that in front of the soundman, grips, lighting crew, script supervisor, camera operators, craft service workers, director, and assistant director? Tom had to do it several times. Do you have that courage?

Jason Alexander, star of *Seinfeld,* had this to say about courage and acting: "There are some people who are scared to death to be in front of people, or they are scared to death to reveal certain things about themselves. But take away those impediments, and I think anybody can learn to act."

Once again, it comes down to finding the courage. Remove your fears and you can learn to act. If you can't trust the man who breathed life into George Costanza, who can you trust?

Don't say you'd do it if someone paid you millions of dollars. That's not courage. There are actors all across the country in small theaters, in workshops, in coffeehouses, and in backyards with video equipment, and they're acting fearlessly. Nobody is paying them millions of dollars. They're just doing it. That's how you get started. You find the courage to do it.

Don't think of people like Robin Williams, Al Pacino, Susan Sarandon, and Julia Roberts as "talented" (even though they are). Instead, think of them as "fearless." As soon as you become fearless, you will share a rare, starlike quality.

Often when I challenge actors to do these tests, they say, "Oh, those are easy. I do that sort of thing all the time." Maybe that's so, but perhaps that's just false bravado to hide the fact that they're too scared to do them. Only they know. I've also had a few people e-mail me and say that they wouldn't do those tests because they are rude. If you're afraid of being rude, then you don't have a future in anything that is creative. To be creative, you can't worry about what others think about you. The most interesting and creative people are those who have the courage to make bold statements without worrying what the consensus says. As Ralph Waldo Emerson once said, "Popularity is for dolls."

I can't stress enough how important it is to have courage in this business. You could even go so far as to say that courage is talent and talent is courage. For a beginner, the two words are interchangeable. Whether or not you "make it" will have something to do with your look and your ability to act, but it will have more to do with your courage and determination. I guarantee it.

My first speaking role with Jim Carrey

When I first started working in Hollywood, I did a lot of extra work between jobs. It's not hard but it takes determination. I was performing in a play at night and doing extra work during the day. That's twelve hours on a movie set during the day and then two hours of play rehearsals at night. Could you do that? You could if you're determined, as I was. I contacted a casting director who cast union films and told her that I wanted work as a union extra. That didn't just come to me. I did that through networking. I had to call strangers to line that up. She got me a role as an extra in *The Mask*.

There were only three extras on that shoot and we all played cops and we all got paid about $120 a day. We were shooting a scene where Jim Carrey gets stopped in the park and searched by the cops. The director needed a cop to search Jim. I maneuvered myself so that I was looking right at the director as he was deciding this. He looked at me and said, "Come here and search Jim." He told me to pull objects out of Jim's pockets and say whatever it was that I was pulling out. I knew that if I said a line I would get paid union wages, and I'd get into the union. That's a union rule. If you speak a line in a union movie, you have to get paid union wages. If you're not in the union and you speak a line, they still have to pay you, and you can then join the union. It's called Taft-Hartley and it happens all the time on movie sets, as I'll explain in more detail later on.

This was tricky because I wasn't in the union, but nobody knew. When the director asked me to do this, the assistant director said to me, "You're SAG, right?" He wanted to make sure I was in the union. If I had said no, then they would've asked one of the other extras who was a union actor to do the scene. What would you have done? I took a chance and said "Of course." After I said my lines, they took me to the production trailer and filled out my paperwork to change my status from "extra" to "day player." This meant that I was now getting paid $500 a day. It also meant that I could now join SAG.

When they took me to the trailer they asked for my union ID, and I told them I didn't have one. They were a little upset about this, but rules are rules and they had to make me a day player because they certainly weren't going to go back and reshoot the scene without me. I didn't feel bad about it morally either because they would have had to pay the same union wages to anyone who said those lines anyway, so why not make it me? And SAG would be happy because it got another dues-paying member.

This didn't happen by luck. I got to that movie set because I was determined. I wasn't waiting for someone to rescue me. Are you determined enough to do extra work and a play at the same time? It takes a lot of energy. I also had to have the courage to step up in front of Jim Carrey and say, "Pick me." Then I had to stand next to Jim Carrey and actually perform the scene. Like I said, they didn't script the lines; I had to make them up. It all happened very quickly and I had to deliver. It's not a huge scene, but to me it was gigantic, and let me tell you that it was a lot more nerve-racking than standing in an elevator and talking to a few strangers.

As an actor, you can never have too much courage. Do these tests and you'll learn a great deal about yourself. You can't go on to step two until you pass the acting tests. If you blow this off and say, "Ah, he's crazy, I don't have to do this to be an actor," then you're fooling yourself. If you really want to be an actor, then you will overcome those silly fears and pass the tests. Once you've passed the tests, then your acting education truly begins.

> I have a lot of things to prove to myself. One is that I can live my life fearlessly.
>
> —Oprah Winfrey

ACTION POINTS

- Making it as a beginner is all about your courage and determination.
- If you want to know if you have what it takes, then challenge yourself.
- You can develop courage and reduce your inhibition by practicing excitation.

DAILY GOALS

Get out that calendar and make a date with courage. Decide which test would be hardest for you to do, then mark a date on your calendar to do that test first. Your goal is to do at least two of the "a" tests and two of the "b" tests. Don't move on to the next step until you've passed. Keep in mind that there's nothing physically preventing you from doing these. The only thing that will stop you is fear, and fear will kill you as an actor.

If you take a particular test and fail, you can still say you did something and that's all that counts. That's still progress. You can always do it again. If you take a test and pass, then you can say that you proved to yourself that you have what it takes.

Before you go to bed, ask yourself "What did you do today to advance your acting career?" If you can say, "Today I faced my fears and overcame them," then you have what it takes to make it and you're on your way to the next step.

5

STEP TWO OF YOUR ACTING PLAN: LEARN HOW TO ACT

By now you've completed step one and you've passed the acting tests. If you haven't passed, then you can use this step to find an acting class that will help you pass. Be very careful about skipping the acting tests. If you find yourself saying, "I don't wanna do that stuff. I just wanna be an actor," then you might be in denial about how courageous or determined you are.

Remember that you need to stay on a focused path to reach your goals. Learning to act is going to require courage. If you can't pass those tests, you'll have a hard time growing as an actor. If, however, you feel that you need help to pass the tests, then a good acting workshop and teacher might be just what you need. If that's the case, then you'll have to go back and pass the tests once you've received the proper training.

As strange as it may seem, the step of learning how to act is often overlooked. Some will argue that it's the most important, while others may claim it's the least important. Meryl Streep studied drama at Yale University. At the time of this writing, Frankie Muniz, child star of the hit sitcom *Malcolm in the Middle,* has not taken any acting classes. Learning how to act does not necessarily mean years of school and lessons. In fact, some say that acting can't be taught at all. Some stars like Will Smith might have no formal training, but that doesn't mean he never "learned" how to act.

I mentioned in chapter 4 that acting is about courage and determination. Will Smith found the courage and determination to become a rap artist. He learned how to act by getting up onstage and singing in front of people. He put in a lot of stage time before his first TV show. A stage is a stage, and it doesn't matter if you're singing or acting. It's all about performing in front of people and the only way to do it is to face your fears.

Who has the ability to act?

> Through practice we develop confidence in our ability to utilize the talent that is there.
>
> —Scott-Arthur Allen, Los Angeles
> talent manager and acting coach

What Scott-Arthur is talking about is our innate talent as human beings. In other words, we all have the ability to act. That ability can vary, of course, but we all have it. By practicing and developing your confidence, you can realize your own ability to its full potential.

Instead of learning to act, you could think of it as simply practicing acting. Will Smith wasn't really learning to act in the sense that he stood onstage and thought, "Hmm, this is what actors do." Instead he just logged many hours of stage time as a musical performer. He was simply practicing his performances onstage. Remember that although many people want to become stars and they think about getting photos, agents, and union cards before they've done any acting, the first thing they need to learn is how to get up onstage and perform. After years on the singing stage, it was very easy for Will to make the transition to TV.

Books to read to learn about the craft of acting:

* *Respect for Acting* by Uta Hagen—One of the most respected authorities on learning to act.
* *Actors on Acting* by Cole and Chinoy—Theories and insights about acting technique from over a hundred different actors from various eras and cultures.
* *To Become a Fine Actor* by Norman Sturgis—An outstanding reference for creative thinking as it relates to learning how to act.
* *The Tyranny of Words* by Stuart Chase—This explains how language controls the way humans act.
* *Conditioned Reflex Therapy* by Andrew Salter—Simply the best book for understanding shyness and other related problems and how to overcome them.

Learning to act isn't necessarily difficult, but it's something you need to be comfortable doing before you even bother with all the other stuff. In this chapter I teach you the importance of practicing. In addition, I teach you how to find a good acting teacher and what to expect from an acting class. I also provide you with some basic knowledge of acting so that you can begin practicing right away.

Why it's important to learn how to act

It should be very obvious that you need to learn how to act, but apparently it isn't. Many beginners confuse wanting to be famous with wanting to act. I've seen actors come into my workshop who've done little or no acting and have little or no training. Some are fantastic. They can jump right in and give compelling, exciting performances. Others are so nervous and shy that they can barely say two words onstage without drinking a glass of water. If you're not capable of giving a confident performance onstage, then you're not ready to move on to the next step of the plan, which involves getting your headshot photo. Here's why.

If you live in a small town and you manage to find an agent or a casting director, you might only have one chance to impress that person. If you walk into a casting director's office and you're shy and don't know much about acting, he'll notice it and won't want to work with you. He might see you again in six months or a year, but he won't want to see you again in two weeks.

If you live in Los Angeles, and you get your headshots together and mail them out to forty agents and get an interview, the same thing could happen. You might have just paid up to $300 for photos, copies, books, and mailings, and now you just found out that you don't make a very good impression on people. Bad planning. The business side of acting will come later. What's important at the start is to get involved in the actual practice of acting. Figure out what you're doing onstage first, and the other things will take care of themselves.

If you just want to audition for a play at your local theater, then run down there and audition. That's as great an experience as you'll ever have. If, however, you're trying to make it in the big city, you should have some practice and experience before you embark on any of the other things, because it's going to affect how others perceive you. One of the biggest misconceptions about show business is that it's all about looks. A great look will certainly help, but fine actors need more than just a look to survive. It's really best to learn something about acting before you attempt to further your career.

Whenever I ask beginning actors to go up onstage and improvise something or to read a script, they're usually lost. They're scared and quiet and they look at me and say, "I don't know what to do." (Some experienced actors do that as well but that's a different story.) If those actors were to go get headshots done and start meeting agents and casting directors, they're not likely to make a great impression. After a couple of months in an acting workshop, that could all change. It won't be because an actor has "learned" acting techniques. Instead, it'll be because he's practiced getting up on a stage and performing in front of people. He has become comfortable and confident. Some have it naturally. Some can learn it in weeks or months. Others may take longer. Here are a few guidelines that will let you know when you're ready.

When am I ready to audition?

You need to get to a point where you feel very comfortable about looking at a script for fifteen minutes and then walking into a room full of strangers and performing that script in a compelling manner. When an actor says a line to you, you have to be able to say your line in a way that sounds natural and convincing. If a director tells you to do the line differently, you have to be able to do it. You also need to be able to improvise, because you won't always get a script. Sometimes, in an audition, you'll be asked to make something up. If you've never been on a stage or in an audition, you might freeze or otherwise do poorly. It's not because you're a bad actor, it's because you simply haven't had the experience of being in that situation. Those are the sorts of things you can practice in a class.

If you can do all of those things confidently and convincingly, then you're ready. If you can't do those things yet, then you need to learn and practice. The length of time it takes to get to that point is entirely up to you. Even if you can do those things, it's still a good idea to get involved in an acting class that allows you to do it regularly. Because once you've practiced for a while, your confidence and attitude will change. Your face and posture will change, too. That could change your headshot. Your voice might even change. Don't get trapped into thinking that you need headshots, résumés, postcards, managers, and assistants before you even know how to learn a script. Get some stage time first.

Acting, like any other skill, needs to be practiced. The more you do it, the easier it becomes. Many actors practice throughout their careers as a way to stay sharp and confident. They aren't necessarily getting better, but they're staying active. Ever notice how smooth Jay Leno looks on *The Tonight Show?* That's because he gets out there every night and does it. Even on nights when he's not doing his show, he's often out at comedy clubs doing his act.

Acting is similar to playing music or sports. The world's best musicians and athletes have to practice constantly to stay at the top of their professions. Acting is no different, and that's why many movie stars keep busy doing plays when they're not shooting films.

Agents and casting directors love training

It can sometimes be very difficult to get an agent if you haven't had any training or if you aren't training regularly. I've known agents and managers who require that their actors stay in an ongoing class when they're not in a production. They know that the competition is tough, and only those who stay sharp have a chance.

It's imperative that actors list their training on their résumés, and I discuss that later in the basics step of Your Acting Plan. When you start competing in the big cities, agents are going to look at the amount of training you've had, how often you train, and with whom you train. I don't want you to worry too much about this. It's important, but it won't make or break your career. I just want you to be aware of how seriously professionals consider training.

Most managers and agents in Los Angeles insist that their actors be enrolled in a regular acting workshop. Auditions can come at any time, and they want you to be sharp.

Once you've made a name for yourself, nobody will care if you've ever trained or if you're in a class. Success is a great equalizer. For the time being, just realize that it's important to practice so that you're confident and ready.

What to look for in an acting class

Whenever someone asks me to recommend a good acting teacher, I'm always hesitant. That's like asking me to recommend a good restaurant. How do I know that our tastes are the same? So instead of recommending specific teachers, I tell actors what to look for in an acting class.

Any acting class has two essential elements. The first is the teacher, and the second is the amount of stage time that you get in the class. When I say the word *stage* throughout this book, I'm not necessarily talking about theater. Stage is a general term I use for performing. It could be in a theater or studio, on camera or behind a microphone. Anytime that you're performing, whether it's practice or otherwise, is stage time. Getting stage time is crucial if you're going to grow as an actor.

There are as many ideas about acting as there are acting teachers. None is right or wrong. I once sat in on a class with one of Hollywood's finest acting teachers, but I just couldn't make any sense out of what he was saying. I also once spoke to a jobless drunk in Los Angeles who had some of the most brilliant and creative insights into acting that I had ever heard. An acting teacher has to help you discover ways to give interesting, compelling performances. If your acting teacher doesn't make sense to you or confuses you, then he's not the right teacher for you and you need to find another. It doesn't mean that the teacher is good or bad. He's just not the teacher for you. A "good" teacher is one who makes sense to you and helps you grow as an actor. There is no right or wrong way to achieve that.

You should avoid any teacher who belittles or berates the students. The process of acting is an art. There is no criteria for what's good or bad. There is only trying. A teacher's job is not to make everyone happy or to tell them that they are all wonderful. Sometimes actors hear things that bruise their egos and that's normal. A good teacher tests your comfort level, but any teacher who tells you you're bad or berates you for any reason is not going to be of much help. Feedback and criticism are one thing, but condemnation has no place in acting or any other art. The best a teacher can do is challenge you to push the limits of your creativity and daring.

Last, you should avoid instructors who tell you to "watch me do it." Acting is a process of discovery. A good teacher will give you instruction that guides you to discover the art of performing. A less effective teacher, who doesn't know how to do this, will simply tell you to mimic her or someone else. You should strive to create, not imitate.

Once you've found a teacher whom you like and understand, it's important to make sure that you're going to get onstage during the class. If you're in an acting class and you spend most of the class listening to lectures, then get out quickly. Lectures have their place, but nothing helps you more as an actor than getting onstage. I'm always appalled to hear from students of the top acting teachers who say that they only go up onstage once in a class. Acting can't be learned very effectively by sitting and listening. Find a class where you spend time onstage, not in your seat.

How to find an acting class

My favorite place to practice is in an ongoing acting workshop. A workshop is a group of six to twenty actors who meet for a few hours each week and practice a variety of acting exercises. The actors each get to perform a few times in each class. This is the best way to practice in my opinion. Regardless of what's taught, if you're getting onstage a few times a night, you're going to grow as an actor.

Just about every theater or community center has some kind of acting workshop. Walk down to your local theater and look at the bulletin board in or around the lobby. You'll see a few ads for acting workshops. Find one that lets you get onstage and practice.

If you live in the big city, you can use a publication like *Backstage* to find an acting class. Your local arts publication will list them as well. Find one that will let you audit. Auditing is basically observing a class one time for free. Most good teachers allow this. Be careful about audits. Some teachers will tell you that they allow audits, but it's just a sales tactic. They ask you to pay for five classes and the first one is your free audit. That's no audit. When you audit a class, you'll get to see what goes on and how the teacher interacts with the students. Pay particular attention to the size of the class and how often the students get up onstage. When the class is over, talk to the students about their experiences. If the class seems right to you, then go ahead and sign up. If it doesn't feel right, then go find another one.

One thing you want to avoid is skipping from class to class every month. If you don't like a class, then you should definitely look for a different one, but to practice effectively, try to stay with the same teacher for an extended period of time. If you go to a new class every month, it's hard to develop a reliable process for acting.

What goes on in an acting class?

Although there are no set rules as to what should occur in an acting class, three basic tenets are usually covered. These include improvisation, cold reading, and scene study. Some classes focus on one or more of these concepts, but others might include all three. There is much debate about the relative importance of these and how they should be taught, but most casting directors will want to see these on your résumé, and they really are good things to practice.

Improvisation exercises are challenging ways to test and increase your creativity. In improv, actors go onstage and make up a situation and dialogue. They assume some kind of relationship and see how far they can push their creativity. Sometimes the teacher suggests a scenario and then leaves it up to the actors to "write" the script. The only thing holding you back from doing this well is your fear. Improv is a great way to explore your range and abilities. Nothing builds confidence faster because it's all you. There's no script or guidance to fall back on. It's also a very useful tool because sometimes you'll forget your lines and you'll have to have the ability to improvise.

I once heard a teacher say that he didn't teach improvisation because most TV shows and movies won't allow you to improvise. I couldn't disagree more. It's true that you won't necessarily be improvising every time you're in a scene, but the ability to improvise dramatically affects your entire persona as an actor.

In my experience, I have always found that actors who can improvise tend to be far more creative, entertaining, and interesting than actors who can't. After standing on the set of *The Mask* and watching Jim Carrey improvise both on and off camera for hours, I can assure you that it's an amazing and very useful talent.

At some point when you're in an audition or an interview, you won't be saying your lines. You might just be talking with an agent or a casting director. Even though you won't be acting, you'll still be improvising. If you're nervous and stiff in moments like this, then you run the risk of making a bad impression. Being a relaxed, creative person, capable of thinking on your feet, will help you tremendously as an actor. Take a moment to review and practice the acting tests. Once these become fun and effortless, you'll be a fine actor.

Another popular concept taught in acting classes is "scene study." In a layperson's terms this means "know what you're doing in this scene." Some actors memorize lines and repeat them like parrots without any idea of what they're truly saying or why they're saying it. Scene study involves analyzing the script so that you understand why you're saying the lines you're saying. Sometimes teachers can go too deeply into this area and start to confuse the actors. Some actors can do it intuitively without much analysis. Finding the right mix is up to you.

It's one thing to repeat lines you've learned from a script, but it's quite another to actually understand what you're saying to deliver the lines with conviction. The only way to do this is to understand the script. Here's an exercise you can try with a scene partner.

Get a scene from a movie or play and learn it with a scene partner. Once you've learned the script, do the entire scene using your own words. You're still going to convey the same thoughts, but you're going to use different words. This will test whether or not you truly "understand" what you're saying. If you're just memorizing lines without any real knowledge of what you're saying, then you won't be able to do this. However, if you truly know what you're saying and why you're saying it, then you'll be able to put it into your own words easily. Once you've accomplished that, do the scene again, using the exact words that the author wrote. Your clear understanding of the script will affect your performance and make you more convincing.

Finally there is the "cold reading." A cold reading is what happens at most auditions. You get a script a few minutes before the audition and you have to read it and act it out as best you can. Actors are not required to know the lines in a cold reading, which is why they get to look at the script. However, actors must understand what they're talking about in order to give the best performance possible.

It can be very difficult to look at a script for the first time and then perform it ten or thirty minutes later. It's not hard to learn how to do that, but it does take practice. Imagine for a second that someone hands you a script. You're going to look at it for ten minutes and then you're going to perform it for Steven Spielberg. You might not have any idea what the scene is. You just have to perform it. How comfortable do you feel about that? Are you ready to do that? If you're not, then you need to practice. A good class will help you practice cold readings.

The cold reading goes hand in hand with scene study, and here's another exercise that you can practice. Get a book of plays from your local library and pick something you've never read before and don't know anything about. Then find a scene and make a few copies for you and your partner. Sit in silence for twenty minutes while you each study it. Then you perform it. Don't discuss how you're going to do it with each other because you won't be able to do that in an audition.

At most auditions, you are handed a script and asked to read with a stranger. Even if they give you some preparation time, they won't tell you who you're going to read with and you might read with a couple of actors. Therefore it's important to practice reading a scene alone and then performing it with a partner.

What's commercial acting, theater acting, and on-camera acting?

These are sales terms. Acting is the process of learning a script and then performing it. It makes no difference whether you're on a stage or in a studio or out in a field. Many teachers will try to convince you that you need to learn "on-camera" acting or "acting for commercials." You can even find classes for "acting in soap operas." Many top teachers insist that acting on camera is far different from acting in theater. They usually say this so that you'll take their class. The best teachers I've worked with agree that acting is acting. You learn your lines, then you say your lines. The minor technical differences of the different media and venues pose no problems for a well-trained actor.

Of course you're not required to go to any kind of acting school or workshop. I simply recommend it. There's nothing stopping you from walking down to a local theater tomorrow and auditioning for the next play. Your fears might stop you, but that's about it. No law says you have to have any kind of training to audition for a part in anything. However, if you're too scared to audition or you simply don't know how to audition, or the people you're meeting keep saying no, then you could probably benefit from some kind of training.

Acting in college

I often receive e-mails that say, "Pete, I'm thinking of going to _____ college. What do you think of their theater program?" I can't respond specifically to such people because I don't know every college acting teacher. I tell them to review the same criteria I've already listed. Of course, that can be difficult in a college because you can't always sit in on the classes before you take them.

Avoid "modeling" schools and other branch acting schools. There are countless modeling schools and other corporate acting schools with branches around the world that claim to teach you how to act or how to model in short and usually very expensive courses. These are generally considered a joke in Hollywood, and most actors are no better after graduating.

Many fine universities offer degrees in theater and the performing arts, and there's nothing wrong with spending four years in college studying acting. However, that's not the fastest way to become an actor. That's not to say that acting can't be taught in college, it's just that the amount of time you'll spend actually acting is relatively small compared with the amount of time you're in school. You might spend an entire semester or more studying the history of theater or set design. That's very interesting stuff, but if you're not onstage, you're not growing as an actor.

Many fine actors have graduated from colleges and performing arts academies, but many other actors have gone to college to hide. I know it sounds strange, and most won't admit it, but many actors will choose a four-year college because that gives them four years to hide out and study. They get their theater degree and become an administrator and never attempt to break into acting. The most serious actors get busy. They get into workshops and go out on auditions.

I don't want you to think that I'm downplaying the value of education. I went to college, but I did not study acting there. College can be a fun and enriching experience regardless of what you do in life, and I think it's especially helpful for actors. It's a fabulous time to absorb information as you socialize and enter adulthood. Jodie Foster, who started acting at a very young age and had no formal acting training, studied English literature at

Yale University. She didn't study acting. She refers to the years between age seventeen and twenty-two as the time to "fill your bag of tricks." In talking about these developmental years, she said, "That is where you figure out who you are. From then on, all of your philosophies that you carry to your work stem from that time." Jodie is saying that you should simply study life and absorb knowledge, and that's where you'll get your ideas that you can later use in acting.

Mindy Marin, casting director for *A Clear and Present Danger* and *Face Off,* has something very similar to say as she states, "Come in with a role other than acting. You can love what you do, but what's going to make you interesting to me is that you have a life outside of acting. You cannot be an interesting actor if you don't come in with a world of experience."

In closing, I can only say that the decision of whether or not you should go to college to study acting should be based on more than whether I or anyone else thinks it's a good idea. There's no right or best way to study acting. It's a personal choice that only you can make.

Think of acting as something simple and natural

Some actors have a strange preconception that acting is a complicated, mystical process that requires intense research and analysis. That's what many teachers would lead you to believe, but in reality, it's very simple and natural and that's how you should think of it. It is true that some actors are more compelling than others, but anyone can learn acting if they're willing.

With the exception of action stunts, acting is nothing more than having a conversation. It's simple communication. That's all any actor ever does. It's one of the most natural things that we do as human beings. Many acting teachers, however, seem determined to make this a very complicated and difficult process.

Think about the last conversation you had with someone today. What happened? Replay it in your mind. Listen to the dialogue. Now compare that with some of the scenes you've seen in your favorite movies or TV shows. Your last conversation might not have been as dramatic as a scene from *The West Wing,* but in terms of what you did, it wasn't much different. It's just a conversation. Try to keep that thought in mind and you won't get too confused.

What if there are no classes in my area?

If you've checked and found that there are absolutely no theaters, no schools, no workshops, and no community centers with acting opportunities, then you pretty much have to move. But even then you can still check out a play from the library and perform it in your backyard or living room. Anybody can do that. You might say, "But, Pete, that's not the movies. That's not what I want." That might be true, but you have to do whatever is available to you right now. That's exactly how John and Joan Cusak got their start, by transforming their yard into a makeshift stage.

You have to stay active, and you must keep challenging yourself to learn. There's no right or wrong way to act. Those who make it are the ones who do whatever is available in their area. If the only thing available to you is a book of plays, then go into your room and read those plays. One thing will lead to the next as long as you stay busy.

A very bad plan

One of the worst things you can do is go out and get headshots and, without any acting experience, try to find an agent. I mentioned that Will Smith had no training, but he had a ton of experience as a performer and lots of name recognition. If you've been sitting in your room, surfing the Net and dreaming about being an actor, then it's unlikely that you'll have the confidence and ability to really nail an audition. Casting directors and agents can sense when an actor isn't experienced, and they'll pass you right over.

Therefore, no matter how long it takes, learn how to act. You need to build your confidence and learn some kind of process that you can rely on to help you deliver a convincing and compelling performance. Don't worry about anything else until you can do that.

Once you feel confident that you can act, then you're ready to move on to step three, the basics. The basics are the tools you need to start finding auditions. Some people are ready for the basics within two weeks. For others it might take two years. Only you can decide, but don't move on until you're ready.

ACTION POINTS

- It's important to practice acting so you'll be ready for auditions.
- If you take a class, make sure that the teacher makes sense to you and that you're going to get onstage a couple of times during each class.
- Fine acting is about telling the truth. It's not about pretending.
- Always do whatever is available to you right now where you live.

DAILY GOALS

Find a way to start practicing acting on a regular basis. I've given you plenty of suggestions for doing it. Make a date on your calendar to find a class of some sort. Open up your notebook to the page for step two of the plan and make some notes about where you're going to look for a class or what other ideas you have for practicing. Once you begin practicing regularly, you'll have a regular answer for the following question, "What did you do today to advance your acting career?"

6

STEP THREE OF YOUR ACTING PLAN: THE BASICS

ONCE you've passed the acting test and you've learned to act, you're ready to go looking for work. To do this you need to obtain six essential items. They aren't terribly expensive, and they can vary depending on where you live, how old you are, and what your experience level is. These items are the headshot photograph, your résumé, contact information, monologue, demo reel, and other promotional material. Before you get intimidated and think that this is going to cost a lot of money and get confusing, let me explain that you won't necessarily need all of these items right away.

I mentioned at the beginning of the plan that sometimes you'll jump around between steps and things won't always be so clear. This is one of those steps. These basic items are going to prepare you for a professional job search. You might not need any of these to get auditions at a local theater. You could appear in theater productions for years without ever getting a headshot or résumé. That's okay, because you're building experience. When you're ready to give it a shot professionally, though, you'll need to put all of these things together.

Your job and your work schedule

Before I get into the basic physical elements that you'll need, I want to discuss your job, your work schedule, and how they affect your ability to pursue a career in acting. Believe it or not, this is one of the biggest stumbling blocks for actors of all levels. If you are going to become a film or TV actor, then you have to be available during the day to go to auditions and shoots. Before you do anything else, you need to consider this very seriously.

Imagine your agent calls you and says, "I have an audition for you at 10:00 A.M. tomorrow." Will you be able to do that? Suppose they call you and say, "I have an audition for you at 2:00 today." Can you make it? Auditions happen during the day. Agents make appointments during the day. Films and commercials are shot during the day. Many independent films are shot on weekends. You need to be available during these times in order to participate. That's why so many actors in Los Angeles and New York are waiters, bartenders, security guards, and temps. These jobs are flexible. These actors' days are free, and if they need some time off, they get someone to cover their shift.

I had a student in my workshop who worked nine hours every day and traveled a few days a week for his job. He spent hundreds of dollars on headshots and then told me he was afraid to send them out. When I asked him why, he said, "What if I get an audition? I can't leave work." I handed him this quote from George Bernard Shaw: "The true artist will let his wife starve, his children go barefoot, his mother drudge for his living at seventy, sooner than work at anything other than his art."

He asked me if I thought he should starve instead of work. I told him that I didn't care what he did with his life, I simply said that he wasn't ready to make the kind of commitment it takes to become an actor. I suggested he try the theater. In theater, rehearsals and auditions generally take place at night and on weekends, so they're more suited for people who can't give up or get away from their day jobs. Theater is also an excellent place to practice and get exposure. You need to do whatever you can. It confounds me when people say, "I can't just leave my job, and I'm not doing theater. So what can I do?" I tell them to make sure they find a job that they enjoy, because that's what they're going to be doing the rest of their lives.

When Jay Leno interviewed Vin Diesel during the premiere of Vin's movie *XXX,* Jay and Vin talked about working while trying to make it in show business. Jay said, "The worst thing an actor can do is make $30,000 doing something else." Once you get dependent on your job and you start thinking about things like CD players and the cable bill and restaurants and nice clothes, then you become bound to that paycheck. When my student said he couldn't quit his job, what he was really saying was, *How can I pay for HBO, a nice car, dinner at the trendiest restaurants, and a cool apartment, if I don't have a regular income?* His desire to have "things" like stereos and cool clothes outweighed his desire to make it as an actor.

> When you're trying to make it as an actor, don't spend your money on material things that you think will lift your self-esteem in the eyes of others. Instead, spend it on making your dream come true.
>
> —Vin Diesel

I once worked with another actor who got a job as a security guard at a movie studio. He shared a house with several others to keep rent very low, and he didn't spend any money on extravagances. He was up for a role that would force him to leave town for two weeks and he said to me, "If I take that role I'll probably have to quit or get fired, but who cares. I'll just get another job if I have to." That's dedication.

If you're a student, get involved in a student play and find out what's available on weekends. If you're the manager of an auto parts store and you work nine hours a day, then find a theater you can audition for. If you want to come to Los Angeles or New York and look for film and TV work, then you need to be willing to work either part-time or night jobs while you're out auditioning. But don't even think about getting headshots done until you decide how you're going to live.

Your headshot photograph

Volumes have been written about the content and quality of the headshot photo, and it can all be very confusing. In this section I clearly explain what you need to know and how to go about getting a headshot. Keep in mind that these are guidelines only. Like everything else in this book, there is no set way to do any of this stuff. Don't let anyone tell you that you absolutely have to do it this way or that way. Whatever way works for you is the right way. Your first headshot will be a learning experience, so don't be surprised if you end up getting a new headshot a few months later anyway.

In its simplest form, the headshot is an 8-inch by 10-inch black-and-white photo of your face. The only thing that anyone can agree on is that the photo should look exactly like you, and it should be the best quality that you can afford. However, there are many things to consider when you decide to get one, and they seem to follow ever-changing trends. You can get borders, no borders, glossy, flat, face only, three-quarter shot, and on and on. Every actor and every agent will give you a different opinion about your headshot. When you're starting out, you only need to get something that looks like you and doesn't look like you shot it in your bedroom with bad lighting. The biggest mistake beginners make is getting a headshot before they even need one.

Has anyone asked you for a headshot? Are you to the point where you can audition with confidence and you're ready to give it a try? If the answer to these questions is no, then you don't need a headshot yet. Too many beginners think that the first thing they should do is get a headshot. When I began acting regularly in college, I was doing videos, independent films, and plays for years without ever getting a headshot. If you get a headshot as step one of your quest to becoming an actor, then chances are that it will sit in a drawer unused for a long time. Then when you finally need it, it'll be out of date.

If you're brand-new to acting and you haven't done anything and don't know anybody, don't let anyone talk you into paying for a professional headshot. Do some investigating first. You can get plenty of theater roles at small places without a professional headshot. If your area happens to have a local agent, then you might consider a professional shot, but you'll find out about that later when you actually contact an agent. If you're a child, then you don't necessarily need a professional headshot because your face and body will be changing each month. In these cases a simple snapshot with a digital camera will do fine when you're just starting out. If you find yourself submitting for auditions and talking to agents who request headshots, then you can think about getting one. At that time, network with the other actors in your area and see what they have and what they paid.

Who sees your headshot and what do they do with it?

The short answer to this question is, "Anyone to whom you send it will look at it." When casting directors, agents, or managers receive your photo, they look at it for a second or two if you're lucky. That's not an exaggeration. They're looking for a general type that they have in mind for the role, but what they really want is for something to jump out at them. If they see something that they like, they might pause and turn the photo over to look at the résumé on the back. They don't care how much you spent and they won't ask. Don't spend a fortune on headshots, but invest enough to get good quality because this is going to convey your persona. You want to look alive.

Just because I say that a headshot should look exactly like you doesn't mean it should be a mug shot. The difference between a good headshot and a great headshot is not in the quality of the paper or film, it's in the quality of you.

Here's what I mean by that: What is your general attitude or aura? Do you even know? I'm not trying to get metaphysical on you, but what is your personality like? Are you smart, sexy, macho, humble, kind, and so on? If you're a creative and courageous person, then you should have some kind of tangible quality that should come across on film. A great headshot not only looks like you, but it conveys that special quality about you. Therefore, when someone looks at it, the headshot will scream, "I'm sexy," or "I'm smart," or whatever it is that you are.

An actor from my workshop showed me his new headshots and told me that his girlfriend had chosen a specific shot. The shot she chose looked like him and it was a very serious, sexy photo. I told him that it was a great photo but that he shouldn't use it. He was surprised and asked me why. Even though the picture looked like him, it didn't capture his spirit. He was a very friendly, humble, all-American kid. He was like a Brad Pitt type. His photo made him seem like a Benicio Del Toro type. If an agent saw that photo and called him in, she would immediately discover that he wasn't as serious and dark as his photo suggested, even though it looked like him.

He chose one of his friendly all-American photos instead. That way, if an agent liked that look and called him in, she would see the same *person* as the photo and not just the same face. By the way, that actor was signed within one month of sending out his new headshots.

If you've learned how to act and you're ready to submit to auditions, agents, and casting directors, and you actually have a credit or two on your résumé, and you live in a city where there are legitimate acting opportunities, then you need a professional headshot. Here's how to do it.

I look at all the headshots I receive in the mail. If somebody's face doesn't jump right off the page, their photo goes right into the garbage. I won't even look at their letter. If you get someone who's just an average photographer, you're probably not going to get the quality you need on your headshot.

—Ed Goldstone,
manager and former agent with ICM

The five-step headshot process

STEP 1: HIRE A HEADSHOT PHOTOGRAPHER

If you live in Los Angeles or New York, simply throw a rock and you'll hit a headshot photographer. If you live elsewhere, check the Yellow Pages or the Internet for a photographer. The print version of *Backstage* lists dozens of good headshot photographers. The best way to find a good photographer is to talk with other actors. You'll have to address three main considerations when you hire a photographer: price, quality of work, and the chemistry between you two.

Prices vary, so shop around and find someone you like and can afford. Don't let price be the only factor, though. These pictures are important. You don't have to pay a fortune, but don't expect quality for cheap. Photographers usually charge you by the roll, which is typically thirty-six photos. The photographer will let

Getting a headshot is a networking opportunity. Headshot photographers work with actors and filmmakers, so don't be afraid to ask them for introductions and leads. You can also help them out by handing out their business cards. Many photographers will offer a free session if you refer a number of clients.

you know how many pictures he's taking for the price. Ask the photographer to explain the whole process to you, and make sure you understand exactly what it costs and what you get for that price.

Some photographers charge extra for a makeup person. Some take the pictures and hand you the film. Others insist on developing the film and keeping the negatives. Everything is negotiable, so make sure you know what you're getting. This would be a good time to discuss a contract, too.

Don't get too worried over contracts with photographers. You don't need to be a lawyer to figure these out. However, if you don't understand anything they say, you should take it to someone who knows how to read it. Typically, photographers give you a one-page contract that states how much you'll pay, who gets the negatives, and what can and can't be done with the images.

Ask to see some of the photographer's work so that you're happy with the quality. Most photographers usually have a portfolio of samples either in a book or on their website. This is the best way to judge them. Because there's no right or wrong way to take a headshot, you'll have to decide if you like the work. It's your face and your money, so you have to decide.

It's important to have some kind of chemistry with your photographer. You're going to be nervous during your shoot, so you need someone who is friendly and helpful. If a photographer is hurried or impolite on the phone, then try someone else. You're

If you're going to visit a photographer whom you don't know, take all the necessary precautions that you would in meeting any stranger. If something doesn't sound right or feel right, then stay away. Be suspicious of individuals who ask you to meet them at an unusual time or in a remote location. No professional will object to your bringing a friend or guardian to a meeting or on a shoot.

paying for this so you want to make sure it's time and money well spent.

I had an actor call me after a shoot with a photographer she'd never met. She picked him on the Internet because he did great work. She had a short phone conversation with him during which she said he was quiet and not friendly. When she got to the shoot, he continued his cold manner and the whole process took only thirty minutes. Needless to say, this actor was not feeling very happy or inspired and she wasn't pleased with the photos even though they were technically sound. Don't make that same mistake. If you don't click with the photographer, then go find another. There are thousands of them out there very willing to take your money.

STEP 2: THE ACTUAL SHOOT

Bring a few different looks with you, because sometimes a simple clothing combination can drastically change the way you appear. Keep in mind that the photo will be in black and white. That means that a solid red T-shirt looks the same as a solid blue T-shirt. An experienced photographer can help you mix and match, but don't turn into Madonna and start changing outfits every other picture.

Try smiling as well as serious poses. If you have a great smile, sell it. Don't think that you have to just sit there frozen. Feel free to talk a bit and stay loose. Laugh, sing, smile, pout if you want.

This is a performance. If you love the camera, it will show. If you're afraid, that will show, too. That's another reason why this shouldn't be the first thing you do as an actor.

If you've been onstage in a class or in a theater and you regularly rehearse and perform, then you'll be much more relaxed and charismatic in front of the camera. If you've never done anything and you walk into a strange studio and suddenly someone's telling you to sit, stand, tilt, smile, and so on, and you're not comfortable doing that, then you're not going to take a very good picture. Your photo session should be fun. It shouldn't be traumatic. If it's traumatic to you, then you're not ready yet. Get back in class and wait until you're more comfortable.

Another important thing. Do not get more than two rolls! If you can't find a decent picture in seventy-two tries, then you're never going to get a good photo. I've seen people get three, four, or five rolls of film, then they waste a week looking at two hundred pictures that all look the same. Don't waste your time and money. You need that time to get out there and audition.

Much has been said about the type of shot. Should I get a bust shot or a three-quarter shot? A bust shot shows you from the chest up. A three-quarter shot might show you from the thighs up. Sandra Merrill, a casting director for fifteen years in Los Angeles, has this to say about the headshot: "If you have a great body, get a three-quarter shot, otherwise there's no need for it." In other words, don't worry about it. Get the shot you want. There is no right or wrong. I have samples of headshots on my website, www.myactingagent.com, so you can see all the various styles.

There's also much debate about a commercial headshot versus a theatrical headshot. A commercial headshot is usually a brightly lit all-American look. A theatrical headshot is darker, showing your more serious, dramatic side. Do not worry about this with your first headshot. You're going to be submitting to mostly agents and independent filmmakers when you're starting out.

The latest trend in headshots is color. In a pile of black and white photos, a color headshot stands out. With the advent of digital cameras, it's inexpensive and easy to get a great color headshot.

Once you get an agent and start working, the agent will tell you if you need a different look or style. For now, just get a good photo that looks like you. The photographer can help you choose. Look at the photographer's work. If there's a particular style that you like, let her know.

STEP 3: MAKE YOUR PROOF SHEET

You aren't going to take your film to the drugstore and get double print glossy photos and a mousepad. You are going to get a proof sheet. A proof sheet is an 8- by 10-inch sheet of paper that has thumbnail-sized photos printed on it. You'll get one or two proof sheets per roll. That is, the photographer will take your pictures and develop a proof sheet for you. She'll then give you the proof sheet and that's it.

Now you have to go through the proof sheet and decide which photo or photos you want to pick as your headshot. This is where actors will talk to friends, managers, agents, lovers, and photographers and ask, "Which one do you like?" If you do this, you're likely to get a different answer from everyone. There is no right or wrong, so pick the one that you like best. Pick a couple if you want, because they might look a little different when you blow them up to 8 by 10 inches.

STEP 4: DEVELOPING THE ACTUAL SHOT

Once you've selected a shot from your proof sheet, you need to get it enlarged and possibly retouched. Some photographers include this step as part of their package. Retouching is okay if it's done tastefully, but don't go crazy with it. Always remember that your photo needs to look like you. Here's what Mark

DIGITAL VS. FILM

Actors love to debate about film versus digital photography. Which is better? The only thing that matters to you is cost and quality. Look at the photographer's work. If it's good, that's all that counts. Whether he shoots on film or disc is irrelevant.

Teschner, casting director for *General Hospital,* has to say about headshots: "It's very frustrating when an actor walks into the room and I look at their picture and I can't connect the actor to the picture. For every audition that they get based on a misleading picture, they're losing out on the audition that they would've gotten as themselves."

In other words, don't make the mistake of thinking that you'll get more work if you make yourself look different in your picture. You'll get less work, because as soon as casting directors or agents see that you're not the same person, they aren't interested anymore. Also, they won't keep your picture on file because they know that that's not what you really look like.

As I mentioned, some actors like to get enlargements of a few shots just to see how they look. That's fine, but once again, don't go crazy and enlarge every photo. It's too expensive. Blow up one or two and pick the one you like best. Once you've had the photo enlarged and you're happy with it, it's time to make reproductions.

STEP 5: REPRODUCTIONS

You're going to need more than one headshot, so you have to get them reproduced somewhere. This will not be done by the developer, and it will not be included in the price you paid to the photographer, either. You're on your own now. The developer creates your proof sheet and your master 8- by 10-inch photo. To get your headshot printed, you go to a reproduction house. These reproductions are often called "lithos," short for "lithographs."

This is the step where you have to get your name printed on the front of the photo, and you have to decide which style you want. The reproduction house will help you pick a font and a style. They will have plenty of samples to show you, and again you'll have to pick something you like. Put your name on the front, but don't put your phone number or address because those might change. That information will go on your résumé, which we'll get to next.

Don't let the reproduction companies convince you that you need high-gloss, high-quality photos. These headshots are all going to be thrown out eventually. They aren't going on the cover of *Vogue* or *GQ*. Just get a decent-quality print with your name printed on the front. Don't print your name in some wild font either. Hard-to-read fonts are a real turnoff and the sure sign

WHAT YOU DON'T WANT TO DO WITH YOUR HEADSHOT

- **Have the photo significantly altered**—You don't want to show up at an audition looking significantly different from your photo.
- **Make it a glamour shot**—This is not a valentine photo for your honey. Keep the makeup to a minimum and don't go crazy with your hair.
- **Have an unreadable font**—There is nothing more annoying than a bizarre font on your photo or résumé.
- **Spend too much money**—You're an actor. You don't have money to waste.
- **Spend too little money**—This is your career you're talking about. You get what you pay for.
- **Get a composite sheet**—A composite sheet is a series of photos printed on a sheet that shows you dressed as a magician, a jock, a businessperson, and a clown. A composite sheet is for models. Your headshot is just a picture of your face.

of a beginner. Stick with a standard font. You want your face to stand out, not your font.

You'll now have to choose how many copies you want. Most reproduction houses will offer pricing schedules based on 100, 250, or 500 copies. It all depends on your market and how active you are. If you live in Tennessee and you're going to audition for a few plays each year, you might only need a dozen photos at best. If you're in Los Angeles and you're going to do mailings every week, then you'll need 250, minimum. Once you get an agent, she'll tell you how many you need to have, and you'll have to have those ready to go at all times.

I never bought more than 250 headshots, because I used to change my photo after every 250 pictures. What you decide to do is entirely up to you. If you're serious about giving it a shot, get a lot of them. If this is your very first photo, then don't get more than 250 because you're likely to change it. You might meet an agent who wants to sign you but wants you to get new photos right away, so don't load up immediately.

How to get your headshot for free

Because the headshot is the single most important tool for getting auditions, you shouldn't sacrifice too much quality; however, for those on budget, here are some suggestions for saving money.

Beginner photographers, like beginner actors, are always trying to build their portfolios. You can offer to do some free modeling in exchange for a photo shoot. If you have an exceptional look, you'll probably have an easy time finding someone who'll work for free. It's possible that you'll only have to pay for the film and developing. I've known actors who designed websites for photographers in exchange for photos.

Plenty of places offer free or low-cost photos if you look hard enough. Most high schools and universities have photography classes and clubs, and students need subjects for their portfolios.

It's true that these might not be the best photographers, but a headshot is not that hard to do. You could ask around at your job. There just might be a fine photographer in your workplace. Most towns have photography clubs. Check the Yellow Pages, YMCA bulletin boards, learning centers, the Internet. You can find these people if you persist and network.

"But Pete, I'm not just going to walk into a college classroom and say, 'Hi, will somebody take my picture?'" Why not? What's stopping you? I told you that it takes courage to become an actor and that's why I asked you to take the acting tests.

When to change your headshot

Don't get impatient and change your headshot every month. As a rule of thumb, I encourage beginners to start with 250 headshots. You'll soon be mailing these to filmmakers, agents, and casting directors, and you'll go through them quickly. If you don't get any responses after 250 mailings, then that's a sign that you need to change your headshot. That doesn't mean you should necessarily do a new photo shoot, but you should at least go back through your proof sheet and pick a different shot.

If an agent calls you in for an interview, it's possible that he could ask you to change your headshot. It's good to have a proof sheet available at this time so that he can help you pick a new one. It's also possible that he'll ask you to do a new shoot. There's nothing wrong with that. However, if he insists that you use his photographer, then you should treat that with suspicion.

If you're in a major market and you're ready for headshots, then getting started in the entertainment business can cost about $300–$500. That's enough to pay for professional headshots, reproductions, and the mailing costs associated with finding an agent.

No legitimate agent can or will insist that you use a particular photographer. That's the sign of a scam. It's okay if he suggests some photographers whom he likes and trusts, but if he insists, you might want to reconsider working with that agent.

I had an actor come into my workshop who had never acted before. After six weeks of classes, he asked me to take a photo of him using a camcorder. I sent him the digital shot via e-mail and he printed it out on his printer. He sent it out to some casting notices and was cast in his first play within two months of becoming an actor. Total cost for this was less than $5.

I had another student in that same class who got conned into buying a complete online portfolio with website and various photos. She paid over $700 and never went on one audition.

It always comes back to how determined and committed you are. You will meet plenty of people who will tell you that your headshot is great or that your headshot is lousy. The person who succeeds, however, is the one who stays focused and does not give up. Once you're ready, go get a good, affordable photo of your face. That's all you really need to know.

Your contact information

This is the easiest part of the process and only requires a few paragraphs to explain. You need to be reachable! Auditions could come at any time, and you have to be reliable. Make sure you have a working phone with a reliable answering machine or voicemail service. Pagers are fine, too, and many agents prefer them along with cell phones because they can get in touch with you at any time. Keep them turned on at all times.

An agent might have to fax you a script or other documents, so you'll need that as well. You don't necessarily need a fax machine for this. There are plenty of free fax services on the Net. You should also have e-mail because that's the way business is done nowadays, and you will not be perceived as professional or capable if you don't have an e-mail address. That's all very simple and affordable stuff.

I read articles about acting that describe how actors have all the latest gadgets, including PDAs and multiple cell phones. A cell phone is great, but if you can't afford one at the start, don't worry about it. Just make sure you're reachable and have a place to live—or at least a place to get your mail, e-mail, and faxes.

Your monologue

Every good actor has a monologue or two committed to memory for a couple of reasons. First, it shows that you're able to learn a script. It's very rare that an agent or casting director will ask you to perform a monologue, but it's not unheard of. In theater, however, you will almost always be asked to perform a monologue as part of an audition. Learning one incorporates all the skills you've acquired as an actor, and practicing one is a way to keep your abilities fresh.

A monologue is a scene or speech from a play or movie in which one actor speaks from one to three minutes. There are entire books that contain just monologues from plays and movies, and even though it's better to know the entire play, these will do. Be careful, though, about picking something that is well known.

Here are some excellent, lesser-known websites for finding acting books:

www.booksaboutacting.com.
www.bookbaron.com
www.freebooks5000.com
www.alibris.com

Nearly every female actor chooses one of Laura's monologues from *The Glass Menagerie,* and nearly every male actor chooses something from Biff or Hap in *Death of a Salesman.* These are outstanding plays by brilliant writers, but these monologues have been performed a million times, and for a casting director who is looking for something fresh, they come across as being hackneyed. Find something new.

I would also discourage you from performing monologues from movies. Two problems are associated with this. The first is that if it's something well known, you're inevitably going to be compared with the actor who made the role famous. Second, you're very likely to end up imitating the famous performance. A casting director wants to see how well *you* can act. She's not interested in your Al Pacino impersonation. If you're going to perform a film monologue, make sure it's either very rare or that you do it in a completely different way from the film version.

Last, I would discourage you from learning a Shakespearean monologue unless you're auditioning for a Shakespeare play. His language is so distinctive and, well, "Shakespearean" that it will be hard for anyone to determine what you're really like.

Having said all of this, I recommend that you choose a monologue from a play. It would be best if it's something that you've read and enjoyed, but it doesn't have to be. Read the entire play so that you understand the context completely. At the beginning of each play, there is usually a list of characters with a brief description. Find a play that has a character of your type. Then read the whole play and make notes along the way. If your character has a speech of one to three minutes in length, make a note of it and get back to it *after* you've finished reading the whole play. This is also a great way to familiarize yourself with theater and dramatic literature in general. There are books of plays in any library or online bookstore. Used bookstores are an especially great source for these.

It's best to know at least two monologues: one dramatic and one comedic. These will often be the types of monologues requested at theater auditions.

Your résumé

The résumé shows what you've done. When you want to get work as an actor, you have to tell people what you've done. It's not always enough to say, "I'll be really good and work really hard. I'm really a great actor. Please give me this role." That technique will work when you're making a backyard movie with your friends, but when you're looking for an agent or submitting yourself to be cast in something a bit more advanced, you're going to need to show that you've actually worked.

The proper format

The entertainment industry is like any other business in that there's no "correct" way to do a résumé. There are things that you should and shouldn't do, but there is no perfect format. Here is a list of the categories you should include, the order in which they should be listed, and what to put in each category.

SECTION 1: WHO YOU ARE AND HOW TO CONTACT YOU

Name: Obviously they need to know who you are.

Contact Information: Don't put an address. This should be your phone number, pager, and e-mail. They need to get in touch with you, and sometimes they need you immediately. If you have an agent, use the agent's contact info.

Description: This includes your true height and weight, and your hair and eye color. Often a very specific type is needed. Don't put down that you're six feet tall if you're only five eight. You run the risk of angering a casting director when you show and she sees that you've clearly lied. You want casting directors to like you.

Union Affiliations: List the unions to which you belong. If you don't belong to a union, don't lie about it. Also, don't worry about it. I'll explain union stuff later.

SECTION 2: FILM WORK

This is where you list any films you've appeared in. You'll list the film title, your role, and either the director's name if he's known or the production company. Do not list extra work. Extra work means nothing to a casting director, and it makes you look like an amateur. If you've appeared in a student film or a film that you and your friend made or any other film that nobody has heard of, do not list the name of the character you played. Here are some examples:

The Mask	Park Policeman	Chuck Russel, dir
Nadir	Lead	Life Force Productions
Alone Tonight	Supporting	USC film

The first entry is a film called *The Mask,* which starred Jim Carrey and was directed by Chuck Russel. Those are big names in a known film, and I actually played the role of the "park policeman," which was a speaking role. The next film, *Nadir,* was independently produced, and I played one of the leading roles, so I wrote "lead." The role and the director are not "known" in the industry, so I didn't include them. In the film *Alone Tonight,* I played a supporting role and it was a student film. If you're in a student film, put down the film school. If you weren't one of the leading characters, put down "supporting."

SECTION 3: TELEVISION ROLES

These are listed just like film roles: You should include the name of the show, the role you played, and the director or production company. Again, don't list extra work, but if you've done any game shows, you can list that. Here's one of my first entries.

The Love Connection Contestant Chuck Woolery, host

You might not think that that's much of a credit, but I put it on my résumé when I was starting out because it was something I actually did and I had the videotape to prove it. Sometimes, casting directors just want to see what you look like on TV and what your personality is like. A good game show can bring that out.

SECTION 4: THEATER

Believe it or not, this is one of the most important sections on your résumé, and one of the easiest to build. There's an attitude in the business that theater is the most pure and challenging kind of acting. Many casting directors studied theater in school and most of them attend theater looking for new talent. Their belief is that if you can do theater, you can do anything — especially act in front of a camera. That's why casting directors love to see lots of theater credits. They prefer known plays, but they appreciate anything. You should list the title of the play, the role, and the theater you performed in. Here are a few of the shows I first did:

Picnic	Hal	San Diego Theater of Innovation
The Rainmaker	Starbuck	Coronado Playhouse
A Night in Natrona	Lead	Fritz Theater, San Diego

Like film credits, you should only list the role if it's a well-known play. If you're looking for work in New York, you could break-down this section into "Broadway" and "Off Broadway."

Many students ask me if they should list school plays. Here are some guidelines. If you're in school, list the school plays. If you're not in school anymore, you can list the school plays, but don't add that it was a high school play. Instead of saying that you did *Twelfth Night* at Darien High School, list the venue as "Theater 308" instead. It looks more professional and it's not a lie because that was the name of the theater you performed in. Try to get all the high school productions off your résumé as soon as possible, especially if you've been out of high school for more than a year or two.

SECTION 5: COMMERCIALS

If you've done any commercials, you should write "Available on request." Do not list the actual commercials or products. If you've done commercials for Coca-Cola and your résumé ends up in the hands of a casting director who's casting a Mountain Dew ad, then you might get denied. That Coca-Cola commercial might've been three years ago, but they won't know from your résumé. If you've done commercials, keep copies on videotape. If they want to see them, you can show them later.

SECTION 6: TRAINING

This is where you list your training. Directors don't care if you've done a day of training in your life, but casting directors and agents love to see training, and they want you to be involved in something currently. TV producers are very hesitant to hire someone who doesn't have experience because they can't risk the reputation of the show with someone who doesn't have a proven track record. You should list the type of training, the instructor, and the location.

Improvisation	Norman Sturgis	San Diego Theater of Innovation
Southern Dialects	Robert Easton	Los Angeles
Drama		University of Texas

Casting directors want to see classes for things like "scene study," "improv," and "cold readings." Those are legitimate areas of study and do have value. Do not list a high school drama class unless you're in high school. Do not list "modeling" schools. These have very little credibility in Hollywood.

Last, if you've just moved to Hollywood or New York, *don't* do this on your résumé:

Acting I—Doug Hoffman Acting School, Stamford, CT
Acting II—Doug Hoffman Acting School, Stamford, CT
Acting III—Doug Hoffman Acting School, Stamford, CT
Advanced Acting—Doug Hoffman Acting School,
  Stamford, CT

It's not that Doug Hoffman isn't a great acting teacher. Maybe he is, but to those in show business, it's obvious that you took four six-week-long acting classes from some local teacher in Connecticut named Doug Hoffman. He might be a legend in your town, but he's nobody in Hollywood, so leave it off. Just put down that you studied acting with Doug Hoffman at the Darien Dinner Theater and put the name of your current teacher at the top of your list. Agents and casting directors are most concerned with where you're studying *right now*.

SECTION 7: SPECIAL SKILLS

In this section, a beginner compensates for lack of training or experience. List the special skills you possess that can be useful to a filmmaker. For example, skiing, skydiving, and singing are all useful skills that could get you work as a beginner. Don't include typing, investing, or computers as a special skill because those things can be faked in movies and they don't need to hire someone with investing skills to play the role of an investor.

Also, don't put it down unless you do it well. If you're a legitimate singer, include that and include the range. If you are a black belt in Shotokan Karate, then write that down. But if you took a four-week course on self-defense at summer camp three years ago, don't include martial arts in your special skills.

The same goes for foreign languages. Just because my wife taught me how to yell at the cat in French doesn't mean I should put down "Some French" on my résumé. Only include the language if you're fluent.

These skills are especially important for commercials. When I was a beginner, I got a role in a country music video because I could swing an ax. I auditioned with a bunch of weightlifters and models who tried to swing the ax, but they just didn't look right because they'd never done it before. I grew up in Connecticut and had learned how to chop wood with an ax. When I took my turn, the director said, "Now that guy looks like he knows what he's doing." I wasn't the biggest guy or the most experienced actor, but I had a special skill and it got me the job. That doesn't mean that I would include "ax swinging" on my résumé, but I do include "pole climbing" and "construction/tools," and they have both been needed skills that got me auditions.

Commercial casting directors are often asked to find someone who can do yoga, ride a unicycle, hang glide, speak Russian, or dribble a basketball with each hand. Think hard about it and you might discover that you have more special skills than you realize.

What if I don't have anything to put on my résumé?

Imagine you've never done anything in the business. This is the first time you've considered acting. In that case, your résumé is your name, phone number, height, weight, and special skills. "Hey, Pete, what kind of résumé is that? That won't get me any

> If someone who didn't have a particular skill could "act" it
> convincingly, then it's not a special skill and shouldn't be
> listed on your résumé. For example, wine tasting can be
> acted and therefore isn't a special skill as far as acting is
> concerned.

work." You're not completely correct. First, it's *your* résumé
because you haven't done anything yet. Second, a résumé like
that won't get you a costarring role on the hottest TV shows, but
that's not what you're shooting for on day one of your career.
Also remember that if a casting director sees something really
special in your headshot, she might not care if you have any
credits at all. I've said before that looks aren't everything, but
sometimes a look can get you in the door.

Your résumé is going to evolve. You're going to build it up and
I'm going to teach you how. Look at these examples of different
experience levels, and then I'll explain how to start filling yours
with roles.

Beginning Résumé

TOM KRATKY

Height: 5' 9"	*Hair:* Brown	*phone:* 555-4321
Weight: 165	*Eyes:* Hazel	

THEATER

The Glass Menagerie	Tom	Grosse Point High

TRAINING

Intro to Acting   Mike Del Sordo   Grosse Point Theater, Michigan

SPECIAL SKILLS

Motorcycle racing, ballet, fluent in French, can walk on hands.

This is what many résumés look like when actors come to Hollywood. If you were a casting director, would you want to hire this actor? A casting director can't meet everyone, so she doesn't know if you're a great actor yet. She has to look at the résumé to decide if she should even give you an audition. Obviously, you're not very experienced, so you don't have much of a shot, but if she needed someone who could speak French and walk on his hands, then she might call you in because being able to do both is a very rare skill. If you're very young, casting directors don't expect much of you, either, because you obviously haven't been alive long enough to acquire credits.

An actor with this kind of résumé shouldn't spend all of his time looking for an agent, because he doesn't have much to offer yet. This actor needs to find a way to get more roles on his résumé. The best place to do this is at a local theater and at film schools and universities that are making movies for free with local actors. I'm going to explain where to find those credits later. With a few more roles, the résumé starts to look like the intermediate.

Intermediate Résumé

MIKE KOENIG

Height: 6' 1"	*Hair:* Black	*phone:* 555-1324
Weight: 185	*Eyes:* Blue	

FILM

The Mask	Park Policeman	Chuck Russel, dir
Nadir	Lead	Life Force Productions
Running Scared	Lead	Life Force Productions

TELEVISION

Hollywood Squares	Guest	Whoopi Goldberg Prod.

The Match Game	Guest	CBS/Michael Jacobs

THEATER

The Rainmaker	Starbuck	San Diego Theater of Innovation
Look Back in Anger	Jerry	Seven Faces Theater
The American Dream	Dream	Coronado Playhouse
A Night in Natrona	Lead	Complex Theater
Ben and Martha	Lead	Seven Faces Theater

COMMERCIALS

Available on request

TRAINING

Intro to Acting	Ralph Perschino	San Diego
Scene Study	Louis Lerma	San Diego

SPECIAL SKILLS

Racquet sports, swimming, surfing, southern dialects, biking, ice hockey, construction/tools, utility pole climbing, yoga, rappelling, football, baseball, basketball.

This guy went out and got involved in a lot of theater. He built up his experience and his training. He also went on some game shows where he won enough money to pay for a really good scene study class and a new headshot. His new training is helping him grow as an actor, and his auditions are improving. He finally got an agent to sign him, which means he gets access to the good auditions that he never heard of before. He's still not going to be on the top of the list, but now his agent is calling the casting directors and saying, "Hi, Barbara, I heard you're casting that new pilot for NBC. I want to send Mike over for an audition. He's great." After he gets called in for a few things, his résumé becomes advanced, like this one:

Advanced Résumé

KAREN MARION

SAG/AEA

Height: 5' 6"	*Hair:* Brown	*phone:* 555-4567
Weight: 120	*Eyes:* Blue	*pager:* 555-8910
	e-mail: kmarion@myactingagent.com	

FILM

LA on $5 a Day	Charmer	Todd Hughes, dir
To the Moon Alice	Perky Girl	Jessie Nelson, dir
The Unborn	Louisa	Rodman Flender, dir
Running Scared	Lead	Life Force Productions
Enough Tonight	Lead	139 West Productions

TELEVISION

General Hospital	Karen Greenwood	ABC
Friends	Delivery Girl	NBC
Austin Comedy Network	Featured	ACN Productions
SBC Customer Service	Lead	SBC

THEATER

Three Sisters	Olga	Craft Theater, San Francisco
The Rainmaker	Lizzie	Craft Theater, San Francisco
Look Back in Anger	Alison	Boston Community Playhouse
Fool for Love	May	University of Massachusetts

Orpheus Descending	Lady Torrance	University of Massachusetts
Romeo and Juliet	Juliet	Boston Community Playhouse
Taming of the Shrew	Katherina	Boston Community Playhouse
Ben and Martha	Lead	Cape Cod Dinner Theater

COMMERCIALS
Available on request

TRAINING

Scene Study	Norman Sturgis	San Francisco
Improv	Norman Sturgis	San Francisco
Southern Dialects	Robert Easton	Los Angeles
Voice-Over	Eliza Schneider	Los Angeles

SPECIAL SKILLS
Racquet sports, swimming, surfing, southern dialects, biking, gymnastics, ballroom dancing, fluent in French and German.

This is the kind of résumé that gets Karen a lot of calls. It might even get her a more powerful agent. Anyone in Hollywood could look at this and see that she's well rounded, professional, and dedicated. If she's right for something, they will not hesitate to call her for an audition.

Stretching the truth

Many beginners want to lie to make their résumé look a little better. Casting directors can spot a beginner instantly, and they'll advise you to never lie about any of your credits. If you lie about a play that you've been in and they ask you about it, then you'll lose what little credibility you have. If you lie about something that the casting director has cast, then you really look bad. Still, there is always that temptation to stretch the truth. Be careful about what you do.

Academy Award–winning actor Jon Voight once said: "It seems impossible in the beginning. You know, we try to make up credits because we don't have much experience. So we kind of invent things to put on our résumé to have somebody pay attention to us."

You can see that even a legendary star like Jon Voight was once faced with trying to get noticed. Many actors do it. If you're going to exaggerate your résumé, make sure you know what you're talking about. If you do put an exaggeration on your résumé, make it your goal to replace it with the truth very soon.

Filling your résumé with credits is not as difficult as it might seem. It can actually be very exciting. All you have to do is stick to the plan. The next chapter teaches you how to find the roles that will make your résumé look good enough to get noticed.

Don't agonize

Last, the résumé should not be something that you agonize over. I've seen actors debate endlessly about whether they should include the director's name or the production company's name. How many spaces should they leave after their phone number? Should they put "surfing" *and* "windsurfing"? Anal details like that are a complete waste of time. Just format it all neatly and include all the pertinent things you've done. That's it. It's really simple. People who agonize over this stuff are missing the real point, which is to get out of the house and go find roles to include on that piece of paper. That's really the only thing that counts.

The Demo Reel

The demo reel isn't something that you need right away. In fact you can't make one until you've actually appeared in something. A demo reel is a VHS tape, CD, DVD, or web video of your work. Demo reels aren't usually more than seven minutes in length, and they contain clips that are five to twenty seconds in length. There's nothing stopping you from putting an entire commercial or play on a tape to show someone, but agents and casting directors don't want to watch your three-hour version of *King Lear* on tape. They want to see a series of short clips so that they can see how you look on tape, listen to your voice, and get an overall impression of you as an actor. A good example of demo reel production can be found at www.demoreels-foractors.com.

> In today's market, every agent wants to see tape on someone, and it can't be some homemade tape of you on your birthday or doing a monologue. It should be a professionally produced reel about seven minutes in length, and it has to look great. I would suggest going to an editing house and have them edit something that looks really sharp.
>
> —Ed Goldstone,
> manager and former ICM agent

As you're doing your plays and free videos and movies, you want to make sure that you get copies of everything. Most students and independent filmmakers are shooting on some kind of digital format, so you should try to get a digital copy. You want to keep a digital master of all the work you've done. This digital source material can be given to an editor to make your demo reel. If you give an editor a VHS copy, the quality is going to get progressively worse when it's edited. If a VHS copy is the only thing you can get, then take it, because it's better than nothing, but try to get a digital copy if you can.

Don't worry if you don't understand the digital formats. The filmmakers and editors understand these. All you have to do is request that it be digital, and they'll tell you what you need to do.

If you've done six student films, hire a professional service to edit five minutes worth of scenes together on a demo reel. Then if an agent or casting director ever asks if you have a "reel," you can show them your tape.

Once you're ready to produce a demo reel, search for an editor any place that you find other acting services. Publications like *Backstage* run ads for demo reels, or you can try a search on the Net using the phrase "actors demo reels."

Other promotional material

There are other promotional items that you should consider, but once again, I don't want you to think you need these things immediately. These include business cards and postcards, and you should really wait until you're in a serious acting city before you even think about these items.

A postcard is made from the same negative that your headshot came from. It's just a copy of your headshot printed on a standard postcard-size piece of card, which is typically 5 by 7 inches. This does not have your résumé on it. It just contains your name and contact info. You send this as a reminder to agents or casting directors to whom you've already mailed a résumé. You could also use it as an invitation to the latest play that you're starring in. This is covered later.

Business cards can have your headshot printed on them along with your contact information. These are used for networking. Whenever you're on a film shoot, at a networking event, or happen to meet an agent at a coffee shop, you can hand these out. Business cards are standard supplies for serious actors in Los Angeles and New York. You can get them printed by the same place that printed your headshots, but as I mentioned earlier, don't worry about doing that on day one.

ACTION POINTS

- Be prepared for the costs involved in supplying yourself with some basic necessities if you want to pursue acting.
- The very first things you need to consider are résumé, contact information, monologue, and headshot.
- Don't worry about the minor details of any of these elements, just work toward putting them together as best you can.

DAILY GOALS

In chapter 7 I'm going to teach you how to find roles to put on that résumé. Some of these will require that you have a headshot and others won't. Don't rush into the headshots if you don't think you're ready. You can continue to practice acting and search for small roles while you're waiting for that photo. Here's what you should do now.

Create your résumé. Follow the format in this chapter and create a résumé. Print it out and stick it on your refrigerator—even if it's just your name and phone number. Do it. Next, I want you to decide what you need for headshots. If you're ready for a professional shot, start researching photographers and set a date to get your photo done. If you're not ready for a headshot or can't afford one yet, don't worry about it, you can still stay busy doing other things.

As always, ask yourself this question: "What did you do today to advance your acting career?" If you started a résumé and found a few headshot photographers, you're moving forward in a systematic way.

7

STEP FOUR OF YOUR ACTING PLAN: FINDING AUDITIONS ON YOUR OWN

Now that you've prepared yourself with the basic items needed to look for work, you can begin your search for your first acting roles with confidence. If you haven't done any of the prep work, then you might be in for a rude awakening, which could include getting scammed, wasting money, and performing badly at auditions. None of those consequences are life-threatening, but they'll stall your career and discourage you. Too many actors quit because they think show business is unfair or too hard. Sometimes the truth is that they just didn't know how to prepare.

Do you want to audition for the next Austin Powers or Harry Potter movie? If you do, then let's begin with a quick review of the casting process from chapter 2. To audition for a major movie, you'll need an agent. To get an agent, you'll need to have a great headshot and some solid credits on your résumé along with a demo reel of things you've appeared in. Listen to what Lisa Lindo Lieblein of Acme Talent and Literary Agency, one of the top agencies in Hollywood, has to say about getting tape of yourself acting: "I look at every videotape that comes in. If some-one has videotape and I mean real videotape, not tape the actor shot of himself doing a monologue, but any student film, any kind of tape at all that's real work—we watch it."

That's great news for you. A top talent agent has said that she'll look at tape of you if you send it to her. I mentioned the demo reel in step three of the plan. Whenever you appear in something from now on, you're going to get a videotape copy. With each new role, you're going to build your demo reel.

So when you're starting out, don't think of going for the big movies. They aren't available to you yet. Instead, you're going to focus on the productions that are available to beginners. By audi-tioning for these you'll be able to gather scenes for a demo tape and add credits to your résumé so that you can get an agent. That's the path you have to think about.

The audition search has two very important parts. The first is finding the actual auditions, and the second is submitting your-self to be cast. This second part might involve a phone call, an appointment, or a formal cover letter. I'm going to cover all of these aspects so that you'll know exactly where to find the roles and how to contact the people who are casting. Don't be dis-couraged if some of these sources don't sound glamorous enough to you. As a beginner, you need to first approach the sources that are likely to cast you. Once you achieve those, they will lead to bigger opportunities.

> Whatever it is, take it. Even if it's the worst dog of a show
> and closes after one night. Take any acting role you can get.
> —Jack Lemmon

This is excellent advice. When you're starting out, you can't afford to be picky. I'm not advising you to compromise your val-ues or your safety, but don't worry if you have to put on a clown suit at a party or spew some awful dialogue in a bad play in front of two audience members. The theme of this book and the guiding force that will help you make it is to *always be doing something.* I'm going to keep reminding you to pursue whatever is available to you right now where you live. The people who succeed are the ones who stay busy. Most actors can trace their routes back to high school theater and even home theater. If you want to be famous like Robert De Niro, then keep in mind that his first role was that of the Cowardly Lion in a school production of *The Wizard of Oz.*

Following is a list of many acting opportunities. Finding acting jobs and movie auditions, like everything else associated with Your Acting Plan, requires patience, persistence, and resourcefulness. I'll show you as many opportunities as I can, and you might come up with other ideas on your own, but these won't simply fall into your lap. You can't read through these and say, "Ah, that's nothing. That's too small. I'm not gonna do that." If you say that, then you're stuck where you are right now. You have no agent and no auditions lined up. If you went to an agent today, he'd say, "Sorry, kid. Gotta have some experience." Actually, he wouldn't even say that because he won't even talk to you.

If you go out and land some of these roles, then you can go back to that agent and say, "Here's what I've done and I have the tapes to prove it." Then he's going to take you seriously and you might get signed.

Here are the main places where a beginner can get experience and gather tape for the demo reel.

Backstage *and* Backstage West

I want to start with *Backstage* because it simply is the best resource available, and every serious actor uses it to find work.

It's a well-respected and comprehensive source of auditions and acting information in general. If you live in New York, Los Angeles, Chicago, Las Vegas, or parts of Florida, then *Backstage* is an absolute gold mine. The print publication is called *Backstage* or *Backstage West,* depending on where you live. The web address is www.backstage.com. Most of the audition sources listed in this chapter can be found in *Backstage,* including theater, film, video, and more. New acting roles are posted weekly. It's almost impossible not to get work if you read this every week.

If you subscribe to the online version, you'll get to post your headshot and résumé on the Net, and you'll also get access to the back issues. This is very valuable because in addition to the audition notices, you can read interviews with actors, agents, casting directors, and others in the industry who can teach you very valuable information. If you're a beginner, and you're not reading *Backstage* regularly, then you're way behind the competition. If you don't live in one of the major cities served by *Backstage,* I highly recommend that you buy an issue occasionally through its website so that you can see what's available in the major markets. You'll be amazed at how many opportunities there are for beginners.

As I look through today's copy of *Backstage West,* here are the categories of productions being cast: extras, nonunion film, nonunion TV/video, commercials, music video, voice-over, union theater, nonunion theater, student films. Don't be too concerned if you don't know exactly what each one of these categories means. If you fit the character description of the role, then you can submit for it.

Many of the roles listed were paying jobs, and many were not. Don't worry about getting paid when you're starting out. Right now your goal is to gain experience. What's important is that hundreds of roles were listed for all types of actors. Here's what one of these might look like:

Uncle Tom

Mack Sennet (dir.) is accepting submissions for *Uncle Tom,* a film about a priest who has to raise four children. Shoot starts Aug. 5. There is some pay.

Breakdown—Jenna: Latina, 25–35, warm-hearted, smart, attractive; Chowder: 30–40, brawny, strong intimidating, karate instructor; Robert: 30–42, handsome, loving, materialistic husband; Donna: 55–75, tough as nails, heart of gold.

Send pix & résumé to:
Mack Sennet
27 Moviestar Ave.
Venice, CA 90291

This tells you that the title of the film is *Uncle Tom.* It's a student film in Los Angeles that begins on August 5. It's important to look at these dates. Casting happens very quickly. If the shooting date is August 5, don't send your headshot and résumé on August 4, because it will already be cast by then. You can learn a lot from these casting notices, so read them carefully. For example, the lead is a twenty-three- to thirty-five-year-old Latina. How many female twenty-three- to thirty-five-year-old Latinas are going to read *Backstage* every week and submit themselves for auditions? There will be many, but they won't all be prepared to send their headshots like you will. If you fit this description, you're already in the running for this role.

The role of Chowder requires a brawny karate instructor. That's not exactly a common type. If you're brawny and can do karate, then you're already at the head of the pack. Last, the role of Donna is a woman aged fifty-five to seventy-five. There aren't many actors in that age range, and the ones who are aren't going through *Backstage* every day.

Here are the audition tips listed in every issue of *Backstage*. They apply to any audition situation.

1. **Do not pay any fees to audition.**
2. **No nudity should be required during an audition even if the role requires nudity.**
3. **No audition should be held at a private residence.**

When you see an ad like this, you're probably going to mail your headshot directly to the director or producer, who might also be the writer and casting director as well. Even though it might pay little or nothing, the filmmaker still wants to make the best film possible. She's going to want the same thing that the professionals want. She wants an actor who is well trained with a professional presentation. If you're following all the steps of Your Acting Plan, you'll know how to act and you'll have a properly formatted résumé and a good headshot. If you haven't done any of those steps, you'll have no way to present yourself, and you won't know what to do even if you did get the audition.

School Productions

I know it's not Broadway, but for many of you, this will be the first and possibly the only opportunity available. If you're currently in school, look no further than your school auditorium. School plays are a great place to get started because almost everyone is guaranteed a role in something. Jack Nicholson did high school theater, and so did thousands of other actors. If you're a twelve-year-old actor from Topeka, then this might be the only thing available. You'd be crazy not to get involved. What else are you going to do? Remember that your motto has to be: "Do whatever is available to you right now where you live."

Imagine that you never do a class play or talent show, and then you turn eighteen and move to a bigger city like New York. Now you want to be an actor, but you've never done anything. That's not a good plan. If, however, you do one class play a year and you enter the talent show each year as well, by the time you graduate from high school, you'll have some solid credits. More important, though, you'll have experience, and you're going to be very comfortable on the stage.

To get involved in a school play, you usually just volunteer. They don't require a lot of experience, and they won't ask for a headshot or résumé. High schools often do Shakespeare, which is great training, and they also enter statewide competitions, which is great exposure and experience for you.

Local Theater

Without a doubt, this is one of the best places to start. The majority of working actors in Hollywood got their start doing some kind of theater somewhere. Local theaters can offer much more than just roles, they can offer a link to all the knowledge you're seeking as a newcomer because local theaters contain local actors, and local actors can tell you all about the auditions and agents in your area.

Theaters generally come in two sizes, Equity and non-Equity. Equity is the union that governs the rules and pay of theater performers. Generally speaking, if the theater has a hundred or more seats, it's considered an Equity theater and has to abide by Equity rules. If a theater has fewer than a hundred seats, it's considered non-Equity and doesn't necessarily have to abide by any rules. These are your small theaters located on the side streets of the artsy districts. If you have little or no experience, there's nothing stopping you from going to an Equity theater in search of work, but you'll have a better chance in a non-Equity theater.

Don't even worry if it's Equity or non-Equity. Walk into any theater and look for an audition. The worst thing that can happen is that somebody says no. The best thing that can happen is that your acting career begins.

Once you get the courage to visit one of these theaters, you can do a number of things. You can find the bulletin board that lists auditions and classes, and you can write down that information and make an appointment for yourself to try out for something.

One of the great things about local theater auditions is that they aren't always prescreened. To audition for a movie, you have to send a headshot and hope you get called to an audition. With local theater, though, you typically just call for an appointment and you get a shot. Even if you don't get a role, it's a great way to practice auditioning.

Another great benefit of doing theater is that casting directors and their assistants spend their nights going to theater scouting new talent. If you can get into a good play at a good theater, chances are pretty good that you might get seen by someone important. However, just getting into any play is great because of the tremendous learning that will occur.

Irish actor Colin Farrell made his leap to stardom with Tom Cruise in *Minority Report,* for which he was paid $2.5 million. Before that big payday, Colin was spotted by actor Kevin Spacey in the play *In a Little World of Our Own* at the Donmar Warehouse in London. Spacey was so impressed by Farrell's performance that he suggested he play the role in the film version of the play. Farrell

Take advantage of local theaters as places to practice auditions. They are usually very lenient about letting people audition. Sign up for auditions even if you're clearly not the right type. This will challenge you to try something different, and it will keep you in good shape for auditioning.

never looked back and is now considered among Hollywood's hottest actors.

Casting directors know how difficult it is to do theater, and they respect actors with lots of theater credits. Also, casting directors and talent agents visit their friends and families during the summer, and they just might show up at The Colonial Theater in Boston on a summer night. If you're in a play there, you just might get discovered.

If you're doing a play in New York or Los Angeles, then you can take the extra step of inviting agents and casting directors to come see you. That's addressed in greater detail in the next chapter, on contacting agents and casting directors.

You can even write and produce your own play. Most small theaters will rent the playhouse to you for a relatively small sum, especially if it's an off night. What you do with it at that point is up to you. I did this in San Diego and Hollywood. I wrote a play called *A Night in Natrona*. Then I rehearsed it with other actors who were willing to work for free. We sold tickets to anybody we could find. We did two performances in San Diego before taking it to Hollywood. We all got exposure, and I landed my first agent. We got more credits, and I can say to people, "I produced and acted in a play in Hollywood."

One of the students in my acting workshop had only been acting for about five weeks when he asked me, "How do I start building a résumé? I want to send my photo to an agent." This

SCAM WARNING!

Look out for vague audition notices. If you see something like "Models/actors wanted for work, call this number," then you should be very careful. This is the way scam artists lure beginners into traps. It could be some kind of salesman or adult movie producer. Stay away from those. A real audition will list the production, the roles, and the shooting date along with a contact name and number.

particular student was learning very quickly because he wasn't afraid to try anything. I told him to go through all the theater audition listings and start auditioning. He took my advice, and within one week he'd lined up three theater auditions. He landed a role at the third one.

That's how easy it was for him to get his first legitimate credit on his résumé. Most important, though, he got a great amount of experience while rehearsing and performing the play. That's much better than any acting class.

To submit yourself for a theater audition might require mailing your headshot and résumé with a cover letter, and that is addressed later in the chapter. It could possibly involve calling the casting director for an appointment. Last, it might just be a matter of showing up on a particular day ready to audition. Theater auditions are listed in local papers in the arts sections. They're also listed in trade papers like *Backstage* and on the bulletin boards at the actual theaters. Check those sources to find something that you could try out for.

When you are actually auditioning for a play, they will usually ask you to prepare a monologue. That's why you need to have covered steps one through three of the plan. They might ask for a dramatic or a comedic monologue. If you have one of each learned and practiced, then you'll always be ready to audition for a play. If they ask you to read a script onstage, then you'll have to fall back on the training that you learned in your acting workshop. You should now start to see the relevance of how the steps of your plan are laid out.

Open casting calls

These excellent opportunities allow newcomers to audition without a screening process. Studios sometimes hold open calls for movies, TV shows, and contests. These aren't a prime source of auditions because they're somewhat rare, but they do happen and you can find them by following the industry news media. Theaters almost always have open calls at some time.

An open call audition could read like this:

> Producer Ray Longoria will hold an open call for *Night Times,* a digital magazine TV show highlighting America's night life. There is pay. Breakdown—Three females and male 21–29, reporter/anchor type. Bring pix. Date and address of studio.

If you've completed steps one to three, then you are ready to submit for this audition immediately. You know how to act, you have a headshot, and you know exactly how to mail it in. For some open calls, you don't even need a professional picture. An open call is just that, "open." Anyone can go. To find these you have to always read the entertainment section of your local newspaper along with any local entertainment-type newspapers. *Backstage,* of course, lists these types of calls, and you should also read the two biggest trade magazines of Hollywood. These are *The Hollywood Reporter* and *Daily Variety.* These publications, also known as "the trades," list all the current news in the industry. Open calls can also be found on bulletin boards of local theaters and on Internet message boards.

Great sites for finding open calls and other audition information:

- www.backstage.com
- www.hcdonline.com
- www.variety.com
- www.hollywoodreporter.com
- www.breakdownservices.com
- www.therightcast.com
- www.craigslist.org

Pick a day on your calendar when you'll spend one hour going through the trades. If you can do it every day, that's better, but for now, just try to commit one hour a week to searching for audition news and open calls.

As I write this, the number one film at the box office is *Road to Perdition,* starring Tom Hanks and Paul Newman. The role of Tom Hanks's son is played by an unknown actor named Tyler Hoechlin. Tyler was found during a nationwide open call by the studio. The filmmakers auditioned hundreds of kids in cities across the country before finding Tyler in Southern California. If you had been reading your entertainment websites on a daily or weekly basis, you probably would've heard about this opportunity, and you could've gone to the audition.

Internet casting services and online auditions

Because I have worked as a webmaster and an actor, I have extensive knowledge about how the many online casting services operate. Thousands of actors are getting scammed on the Net, however, because they don't understand the casting process; thus, they are easily misled by cleverly worded ads for pay websites. For a thorough explanation of common Internet scams, see appendix A.

Two types of useful casting websites are available to actors. The first is the simple free postings, and the second is the low-cost listing services. Free casting sites vary from region to region. Some excellent regional sites include www.craigslist.org, www.jacneed.com, and www.my8x10.com. These sites offer many free audition listings for beginners. These will typically be student films, independent films, and theater, but it's not uncommon to find paying gigs through these services.

Some audition listing services charge a low monthly fee to access auditions. Typically these fees are $10 a month or less. In exchange, you'll be allowed to upload your headshot and photo, and you'll gain access to the weekly list of legitimate casting notices. You'll even be able to submit to some auditions directly online. Two of the most popular include www.backstage.com and www.therightcast.com.

"But Pete, I've been told never to pay for auditions." That's partially correct. You should never pay for the *right* to audition. If a service requires that you pay a fee to audition, then it's a scam. Sites like backstage.com and therightcast.com are not holding auditions; they are simply providing lists of legitimate auditions. It's then up to you to submit yourself to these notices. These sites have a good name and a good reputation. They don't sell hype and that's why real filmmakers post auditions on these sites.

If you're in a small market, you should stick with the free listings. If you're in a major city that is covered by one of these pay services, then you could consider subscribing to the audition listings.

Once you've acquired an agent and joined the union, you could consider joining a legitimate online database service. A legitimate database is available to union actors only, and a fee is required to get listed. There are three such services that are considered the leaders in the industry. The service in Los Angeles is called the Academy Players Directory, www.acadpd.org. In England it's called The Spotlight, www.spotlightdc.com. In New York it's called Players Guide, www.playersguideny.com.

Regardless of how you find an audition, one rule remains. You have to live in the area where you're auditioning. If you live in Illinois, don't sign up for an online casting service that lists auditions in New York because you won't be able to go. Stick with the services that serve your area.

These aren't going to be a prime source because casting directors usually use services like these as a last resort. However, if they do need to look through a database for actors, these are the services they're likely to use. That's why I recommend it in step six once an actor has an agent and has joined a union. These aren't services you need to get involved in when you're just starting.

Extra work

I highly recommend working as an extra, or "background" as it's sometimes called, because it's one of the most effective ways to learn about the business while networking and making money. Extras are all those nonspeaking actors who appear in the background of commercials, movies, and TV shows. Don't think of extra work as a career move; instead, think of it as a learning resource.

If you don't know much about how films are made, then work one week as an extra, and you'll become an expert. You'll get to see exactly what the director does, how she works with actors, and how the camera operator works. You'll learn the relationship between the assistant director and the crew. You'll see how long everything takes and how much work goes into a movie. You get the added bonus of being able to watch a star up close. The best part is that you get paid for this.

Networking is really one of the best reasons to work as an extra. You'll quickly discover that all the other extras are actors, filmmakers, writers, and other show business types who are getting started are just like you. These are exactly the kind of people you need to talk to about auditions, headshot photographers, apartments, acting teachers, and other leads. Typically, during extra work, you'll stand around for most of day waiting to do something. Use that time to talk to people and learn about the industry. Anytime I ever worked as an extra, I always met other actors who were writing or shooting films on their own. In 1989 Matt Damon and Ben Affleck both worked as extras on the film *Field of Dreams.* Imagine if you had been networking that day. You can meet some very talented and helpful people while working as an extra. Get those phone numbers.

If you're in a large market, you can sign up with an extras casting service and you can probably work steadily. If you're in a smaller market, check with the local casting director. The smaller markets typically can't provide steady work as an extra as opposed to a place like Los Angeles where you can get extra work nearly every day if you really hustle.

For more information on how to work as an extra, see appendix C.

Universities—Even if you're not a student

When I tell people to go to universities to look for acting work, they sometimes say, "I'm not a student there" or "I'm not in the drama department." It doesn't matter in this case. Most universities have a TV or film department as well as a drama department. Don't go to the drama department unless you're enrolled in the university. They won't let outsiders into their productions. In the film and TV departments, however, they need people like you, and they'll welcome you with open arms. These students are making short films, commercials, spoofs, music videos, and news shows every week. Each student has to do one to four projects in a semester. That means there are plenty of roles. They can't act in them because they're running the lights and cameras. Therefore, they have to find actors outside of their class, and they don't always use *Backstage* to post their notices.

If you go to the film department and find a class or bulletin board, you're almost guaranteed to find a role. They won't pay you, but they'll give you a copy of the show that you can then add to your reel, and you'll get a new credit on your résumé. Don't overlook this area. This is easy and fun work. One of those students just might end up getting a film deal some day. If you make a good impression, chances are that you'll be remembered. Best of all, though, you'll be getting practice in front of a camera.

When I went to the University of Texas, I wanted to try acting, so I went to the communications building and saw a post on a bulletin board that said: "News Anchor needed for student TV show." I called the guy and said I'd like to do it. He said, "Great, can you be there Thursday from one to three with a nice jacket?" That was the audition. I went to the class and they were doing a simulated news show. I sat down at the desk and they turned on the lights and let me practice reading the story. I was nervous, but I had fun. After the class, two other students asked me if I would appear in their news shows the following week. Within one month I had a reel of four different news shows under my belt. Did that get me a role in Hollywood? No, but it gave me valuable time in front of a camera with others watching.

Recently, one of my students visited the USC school of cinema and just walked around until he found some filmmakers in one of the classrooms. They showed him a large notebook where they kept headshots and résumés of actors on file. He gave them his headshot for the book, and he was called to audition for three films in the first month alone.

Dear Pete, I just wanted to let you know that I took your advice and went over to the studios at NYFA. I met two filmmakers and I'm now acting in my sixth film in two months. Thanks again.

—Charlotte,
London, England

Film Schools—Even if you're not a student

Ever hear of New York Film Academy, American Film Institute, New York University Film School, or the Los Angeles Film School? These are just some of the many film schools where students are shooting movies every day. These filmmakers need actors to make their movies, and they aren't particularly picky about experience. Here's what you do: Go to one of these film schools and find the local bulletin board. You will find messages for crew needed, actors needed, and any help needed for all these films that are being made. Call these people and tell them you're an actor.

Once you get on the set, you'll meet everybody and you'll talk to the actors. You'll become friends with the filmmaker. After the first day, everyone will know you're an actor, and they will all tell you about other opportunities and how they'd like to call you because you're perfect for another project that they're working on. If you find one of these schools, I guarantee you could be on a film set within one week, networking and lining up your next opportunity.

If they don't have casting notices posted on a board somewhere, just ask around. Talk to the people who are there. You can't be afraid to do this. If there aren't any casting notices, see if there are any announcements for screenings, parties, meetings, or anything else. Get together with these people and you'll find yourself in a film before you know it.

Make your own

With the advent of digital filmmaking, practically anybody can make a movie, and many people are making exciting films. Look at the success of *The Blair Witch Project*. One of the most profitable films of all time was shot mostly on video. Many filmmakers are making the switch because it's so cheap. A multitude of places exist on the Net where you can learn about this creative community. The most widely known showcase is www.ifilm. com. In addition to posting all the latest movie news, this web-site shows short films from unknown filmmakers. There's usually a place to contact the filmmaker. You can e-mail the filmmaker and tell her that you're an actor who wants to help out.

Inexpensive filmmaking classes

Many small colleges and community colleges offer digital film-making courses that are extremely cheap and only last a couple of months. Basically you'll be in a class with ten to twenty students, and you'll all have to make a couple of short films. If you're not making the film, then you can act in it. You might end up acting in four to five films in a few months, and you'll practically have a full demo reel. Plus you'll get to learn editing, and you'll make friends with a bunch of other actors and filmmakers.

Entertainment headlines

I've already mentioned this a bit while talking about open calls, but it's worth mentioning again because you need to know what's going on in the industry. I urge you to try to read a few articles every day or every week and see what kind of movies are being made and with whom.

For example, here's a typical headline: "Star Productions to Shoot Ice Hockey Film in Wisconsin." You used to play hockey and you have a friend or relative who lives in Wisconsin. Or maybe you live in Wisconsin. Here's what you do next. Send your picture, résumé, and a brief cover letter to Star Productions. Hollywood will not fly all the minor characters out to Wisconsin. They'll need to do some local hiring. If you get your photo into the hands of the producer or casting director, you could have a good shot at getting hired.

State film commission

Los Angeles isn't the only place where films are made. Every state has a department of film production that lists information about the films being made in the area. This is a great place to start looking for production companies, agents, casting directors, and other film-related information. With a little bit of research, you'll be able to find out what's being made in your area. If there's something appropriate for your type, you can submit your headshot, résumé, and cover letter for consideration.

Open Mic Night

Many comedy and cabaret clubs host open mic nights. Find out when they are and call the club to ask how you get on the list to perform. It doesn't necessarily have to be comedy, either. I have performed at open mic nights in comedy clubs, coffee shops, and bookstores. These are great places to practice because you're right there onstage in front of a live audience. It takes tremendous courage. The crowds vary in size and enthusiasm, but regardless, it's a great opportunity to get some exposure. Just call the club and tell them you want to get on the list. Performers like Drew Carey, Jimmy Fallon, Rosie O'Donnell, Jerry Seinfeld, and Jay Leno all started out this way.

Corporate/Industrial Video

Do you work for a company that does in-house video production? If you do, ask them for a part in the next corporate video. Training videos are often called "industrials," and there's a big market for them.

I worked for a cable company in San Diego that was shooting a training video for workers who had to climb telephone poles. I was a good climber and most of the guys in that line of work were too shy to volunteer. I jumped at the chance and spent the whole day starring in a video. I went on to shoot four more videos with that company. When I worked for Pacific Bell in Los Angeles, I made it known to some people that I was interested in acting. When they were looking for employees to participate in a video shoot, my supervisor volunteered me. It turned out to be a great piece of video for my reel, and it was yet another credit that I could put on my résumé.

Contests

The trick with contests is finding one that is legitimate. As I write this, Warner Brothers and a company called Clean and Clear are sponsoring a contest for young actors. The contest requires that two actors, ages fifteen to twenty-five, videotape themselves doing an acting scene. The winner will receive $5,000 and a guest appearance on a TV show.

These things can be found by visiting television network websites and by reading entertainment magazines. Of course the chances are slim, but it's another opportunity for an unknown to get a break. If you're the kind of person who finds something like this and enters, then you're probably going to succeed at something in life because you keep trying. If you're the kind of person who sees an opportunity like this and says, "Why bother? I'll never win that stupid contest," then you're probably not going very far as an actor. You have to take every opportunity that you can if you want to make it.

In the summer of 2002 the biggest entertainment event of the year was a TV show called *American Idol*. Amateur singers from across the country entered local contests and competed for a chance to win a $2 million recording contract. The judges did not go house to house and recruit people. The only way to enter was to actually go to the local auditions. Kelly Clarkson from Texas sang her way to the top, and she became an overnight superstar. It was the most talked-about event of the summer, and the others who competed, even though they didn't win, got exposure and jump-started their careers. This all happened because they had the wherewithal to find the audition and the courage to go to it.

Public Access TV

Ever see those awful cable shows on those obscure channels called public access? You can get parts in those shows very easily. You can even produce your own. Here's how it works. Cable companies usually have what's called a public access division that works just like your public library. You can go to your local cable company and take a free course that usually lasts one or two nights. During this course, they'll teach you how to use cameras and editing equipment. That's right, they'll teach you how to make a show.

Once you pass the course, you can check out the equipment for free and shoot whatever you want. If you put together a show that meets the station's technical requirements, they'll

Network television websites for game shows, reality shows, and other contest information include the following:

- **www.abc.com**
- **www.cbs.com**
- **www.nbc.com**
- **www.fox.com**
- **www.thewb.com**
- **www.upn.com**

show it on public access and you can call your friends and say, "Hey, turn on channel 57 and see me on TV." Or you can simply shoot yourself doing a dramatic scene, put it on your reel, and say that it was a student TV show. For example, I shot, edited, and acted in a show called *The Austin Comedy Network* in Austin, Texas. We had a blast doing it, and we actually made a few decent programs.

When I moved to San Diego, I got certified to use the public access equipment there and produced an entire play, which aired locally in San Diego. Most people don't realize these opportunities exist. The reason they're available is that cable companies have to sign agreements with cities in order to do business in that city. As part of the agreement, the city usually asks that the cable company set aside a channel and an opportunity for local programming. Because most people don't know about this, the cities usually end up showing city council meetings and other boring stuff. If you have the courage and determination to go down to your local cable company and ask, then you'll find a terrific resource at your fingertips. A great website for finding public access information is www.openchannel.se/cat/.

Game Shows

Don't laugh; these are fun and you'd be surprised where they can take you. I have appeared on *The Love Connection, Hollywood Squares, Match Game,* and *Burt Luddin's Love Buffet.* My total take from these shows was more than $14,000. All I did was answer an ad in the *Los Angeles Times* for "game show contestants wanted."

The auditions are all the same. You take a quick general knowledge test, then you play a miniversion of the game with the staff and other hopefuls. You know what they're looking for? They want someone who's fun and outgoing. Basically, they want people who could easily pass the actor's tests. They want excitement. Watch a game show contestant closely, and you'll notice the constant smiling, cheering, and ridiculously upbeat attitude.

After I appeared on *The Hollywood Squares,* my friends all said, "Hey, how'd you get on there?" I said, "I just went down and auditioned. Here's the name and number of the recruiter." The recruiters always want you to recommend friends. I told five friends, but only one had the courage to go down and audition. Guess what. He got on the show and won a trip to Fiji.

It's all about being fearless. I was auditioning for a role in an independent film and the director was looking over my résumé. I sat nervously in silence while he looked it over. After a few moments, he looked up and said, "You were on *The Love Connection?* What was that like?" I couldn't believe it. We started talking about my *Love Connection* date. It was a great icebreaker, and I did a super audition after that. Anyone who ever appeared on a game show has one thing in common: the courage to audition.

If you have the courage, then start looking in these places. Newspapers like the *Los Angeles Times* advertise for game show contestants in the classified section. At the end of the game show, a number or address will usually appear for contestant information. You can also visit the websites of the television networks. Reading the trade magazines like *Backstage* will also help you find these.

Reality Shows

When reality shows burst onto our television screens, they opened the floodgates of opportunity for many hopefuls. *Survivor, Big Brother, Blind Date, The Bachelor, Fear Factor,* and countless others swept the nation quickly. It seems like a new show comes out every month. These are nothing more than open casting calls for courageous actors. And they don't always want the best looking or most "talented"; they simply want the most interesting. These can put you on the fast track to cash and acting opportunities.

Not only are the actors getting discovered, they're also winning huge amounts of money. Each show raises the stakes to become more exciting, and that means more opportunities for you. If you make a big splash on one of these shows, you're practically guaranteed to get an agent because everyone will be talking about you. You can find these opportunities by visiting the network television websites.

Local Church

Do you attend church? Most churches put on theater productions, especially at Christmas. Some are better than others, but it all adds up to experience. You can put on your résumé that you played Bob Cratchit in *A Christmas Carol* and you'll be respected for having done theater.

Actors Showcases

These are typically held in Los Angeles and New York. Quite a bit of controversy surrounds the way these showcases are organized, but they do exist and they're something to consider.

Here's how they work: A showcase organizer gathers a group of casting directors and talent agents for a showcase night. Then the organizer charges you a fee to perform at the showcase. You'll usually have to audition to be in one, and you'll have to rehearse a scene or monologue of somewhere between two to five minutes in length. You perform in front of all these industry people and if they like you, they can ask to meet with you.

This isn't something that I would recommend for a true beginner because you don't want to get up there and blow it in front of a bunch of agents and casting directors. This is something to consider once you have a bit of experience and know a very good scene to perform. The good side, though, is that it puts you directly in front of the people you need to meet, and many good agents and casting directors attend these events. You can find these listings through *Backstage*.

Cruise Ships and Theme Parks

It might not be Shakespeare in the park, but it's something and it pays. Cruise ships and theme parks are always looking for singers, dancers, and other performers. *Backstage* and *The Hollywood Reporter* are always listing ads for these jobs. It's stage time, and before you think it's a waste of time, think about the story of Eric Gunhus, who is currently starring in *The Producers,* which, as of this writing, is the hottest show on Broadway. He got his start as a singing cowboy in Disneyland's *Golden Horseshoe* revue.

A cruise ship might sound like a cheesy opportunity, but don't be so quick to judge. Casting directors and agents have a lot of respect for people who can sing and dance and do live performances. If you were to book a cruise and then do ten shows or more per week, you'd gain an incredible amount of experience. And there's always the outside chance that a retired talent agent might be on that cruise and will be so delighted to call his daughter, who now works at the agency, and say, "I just met a delightful young actress that you must meet." Stranger things have happened.

Talent conventions

These are a very touchy subject because they are so rife with scam artists, yet Katie Holmes, star of *Dawson's Creek,* has admitted that she was discovered at a talent convention. Before you rush out to sign up, I want to remind you of three very important points.

Make sure this isn't the first thing you ever try as an actor. That is, make sure you've gone through the steps of the plan first so that you know how to act. Also, make sure you check the credibility of the convention and the people there. Last, if you enter one of these, make sure you're prepared to move to Los Angeles or New York because the best thing that can happen is that an agent will say, "You have talent. Call me when you move to Los Angeles or New York."

Submitting for auditions

While searching the Internet and publications like *Backstage,* you'll find that at some point you'll have to submit yourself to the audition. This will involve sending your headshot, résumé, and a brief cover letter to whoever the contact person is. It could be a casting director, producer, or director. Regardless of who gets it, here's how you do it.

Let's start by looking again at a typical audition notice.

Uncle Tom
Mack Sennet (dir.) is accepting submissions for *Uncle Tom,* a film about a priest who has to raise four children. Shoot starts Aug. 5. There is some pay.

Breakdown—Jenna: Latina, 25–35, warm-hearted, smart, attractive; Chowder: 30–40, brawny, strong intimidating, karate instructor; Robert: 30–42, handsome, loving, materialistic husband; Donna: 55–75, tough as nails, heart of gold.

Send pix & résumé to:
Mack Sennet
27 Moviestar Ave.
Venice, CA 90291

The first thing you need to look at are the roles. This notice lists three characters. If you're anywhere close to one of these, then you can submit. The filmmakers sometimes change their minds or alter things, so if you're close, go for it. Don't worry about your actual age. You need to decide how old you look in your headshot because that's what they're going to see. That's another reason why your headshot has to look like you. You don't ever want to send a letter that says, "I know you're looking for a twenty-five-year-old, but I look a lot younger than my photo." That's just plain dumb. If you don't look like your headshot, then get a new headshot.

Next, you need to look at the date. As I mentioned earlier, you need to get this in well before the filming date. Typically, if an audition listing is more than a week old, forget it because it's already been cast. That's a reason why you need to check audition notices regularly. They all have deadlines. If you've missed the deadline, don't bother.

Assuming you're available, you're on time, and you match one of the character descriptions, it's time to submit. You now staple your résumé to the back of your headshot just like you learned to do in step three of your plan. You now need to write a cover letter to the contact person. This should be very brief. It says in the notice that you should send pix and résumé to Mack Sennet, so type or handwrite a neat letter and address it to Mack Sennet. Here's what you'll add in the letter:

Dear Mack,

Please consider me for the role of Chowder in your film *Uncle Tom*. As you can see from my résumé, I have ten years of experience as a karate instructor. I'm currently studying at the Acting Naturally workshop in Hollywood, and I'd appreciate an opportunity to audition for you. Best of luck with the project.

Regards,
Pete

That's all you need to include. They don't have the time or desire to read long letters. You don't want to waste time restating your résumé either. I only mentioned the karate training because it's a pertinent highlight. They'll see your résumé, so you don't need to tell them everything you've done in your letter. Also, don't embarrass yourself with cheap sales talk about how hard you work or how you've always wanted to be an actor. Keep it brief and professional. Your headshot is going to do most of the talking.

Put that letter along with your headshot and résumé into a 9 by 11 envelope and mail it to the address provided. If you want to hand deliver it, that's fine, but don't waste time with small talk when you get to the office. Just drop it off and leave.

Track your submissions

Whenever you submit something, keep a record of it. This will help you keep track of what you're doing, and it will also help

Casting directors hate it when you don't know what you're submitting for. The role should be stated in your cover letter and even on the envelope. And don't lick that envelope. Just use the clasp. They'll like you more if they don't have to tear the package open in order to see you.

build a network of industry contacts. You can use a simple piece of notebook paper or you can do this in a computer file. Just write down the contact information and what you submitted for along with the date you submitted. Keep this in your acting notebook in a section called "Auditions."

You will not hear from most of these people because actors simply don't get called for every role for which they submit. If you don't hear from anyone within a week, you probably didn't get an audition. Don't call them and ask them how it's going. If they want you, they'll call you. If you start calling them, you'll be identified as a pest. Don't feel bad if you didn't get called.

Once you've submitted for an audition, just assume you'll never hear from them again. Keep that record in your notebook because even if you don't get called, if you stick with it, you'll soon have a notebook filled with the names and addresses of lots of filmmakers. Those names will become valuable networking tools later. You might change your look or book a role that changes your experience and résumé significantly. If that happens, you can go back through your auditions section and send new headshots to all those filmmakers to whom you submitted in the past. Many of them will be working on new projects and you just might find a role for yourself.

When you get called for an audition

When you get called for an audition, open your notebook and find the entry for that submission. Take notes and make sure you know where it is, when it is, and what you need to do. Now you have to actually go to the audition.

Many books and essays have been written about what you should do at an audition. I've actually read things that tell you how to shake hands and what to say. I'm not going to tell you how to act. These are all things you need to learn in an acting workshop. Keep in mind what I said about learning to act. There's no right or wrong way to do it. You need to be confident that you can walk into a room of strangers and give a great performance. There's no particular way to learn how to do that, but I would recommend a regular acting workshop so that you can practice.

A final word of warning

I've mentioned it before, but I want to repeat it because so many beginners get scammed, cheated, and otherwise taken advantage of by disreputable people in the industry who often prey on eagerness and naïveté One of the hardest scams to avoid is the one that sounds too good to be true. In Los Angeles especially, ads run every week in various publications that read something like this: "Photographer seeks models, actors. Call this number." Others might say, "Get on TV today, call now." These ads are almost always either for pornography or some kind of setup for a sales pitch. You'll go in and they'll try to sell you a modeling portfolio or acting lessons, or they'll want you to take your clothes off. Stay away from them.

Backstage is very strict about how ads must be worded, and you won't see something like that in their casting notices. Other publications and websites aren't as discerning though, so be careful. If something doesn't feel right, then it probably isn't. As always, the best defense is education. By studying books like this and networking with other actors, you'll save yourself a lot of money and heartache, because it's hard to scam an educated consumer.

Get on a submission schedule

Now that you know where to look for auditions and how to submit, I strongly suggest that you get on a schedule. If you're going to use *Backstage,* then buy it on the day that it comes out and go through it all that night. Currently it comes out on Wednesdays. If you wait until Monday to get it, you'll miss the deadline for many of the auditions. Make it your goal to go through it by Thursday and to submit at least one to five résumés every week. Some weeks you might submit ten to twenty, but start with something that you can do regularly. If you continue to do this as you're attending classes, you'll soon start to get calls to go on auditions, and you'll begin to build credits.

If *Backstage* is not available to you in your area, then look at the other sources in this chapter that are. If you're in a small town, you'll have more success at school or in a local theater. Make it a point to check your state's film commission website once a week for news. Read your local arts publication every week. Check the entertainment websites and trade magazines once a week. Plenty of roles are out there. If you prepare yourself properly and search these sources regularly, then you'll be at the top of the list when it comes time to pick talent.

It's a numbers game

A top insurance salesman once said to me, "Pete, sales is a numbers game. I have to hear a hundred 'nos' before I hear a 'yes.' If I didn't hear a 'no' today, then I didn't talk to enough people. Every time someone says 'no' to me, I thank them because they just brought me that much closer to my next 'yes.'" When you're looking for acting opportunities, you might have to hear a hundred nos before you hear a yes. That's why I'm giving you all these various sources to choose from.

ACTION POINTS

- As a beginner, you're not immediately looking for an audition to be on a hit sitcom. Instead, look for roles that will build your résumé to help you get an agent.
- Don't be too picky. Every acting experience will help you in some way.
- Get on a regular schedule of searching and submitting.

DAILY GOALS

With all of these opportunities, there is nothing holding you back from getting parts and filling your résumé with credits. I have two specific goals for you at this point. First, I want you to go through this list and find at least three sources for auditions that are available to you. Don't be too concerned with getting film roles or paying jobs. At this point you just need to get anything.

The second thing I want you to do is audition for a play. Most theaters will let you audition without showing a headshot first. Try to find a theater audition that you can go to even if you're not ready or right for the role. Don't worry about what anyone thinks. Just go do it for the experience. You'll find this to be a very exciting answer to your favorite question: "What did you do today to advance your acting career?"

8

STEP FIVE: CONTACTING AGENTS AND CASTING DIRECTORS

Part 1: Contacting Agents

Everything you've done up to this point will help you in your quest to meet an agent or casting director. You've completed the basics and now you're looking for roles on your own, and you're submitting yourself regularly. You should now have plenty of sources for finding your first roles and building your résumé. You might stay at step four for months or years, depending on how vigorously you pursue it and what kind of success you find. Don't be too quick to start approaching agents until you have some kind of experience. The more credits and experience you have, the better off you'll be. If you want a good agent, then you have to prove that you're a good actor.

If you're doing your regular audition submissions and you've actually landed a few roles, it's time to add to your already busy schedule. You're now going to add agents and casting directors to your list of weekly activities. Even though you now have numerous sources for finding auditions on your own, an agent has access to more and better auditions; therefore, you want to enlist an agent to help you. You'll approach casting directors, too, because they're the ones who provide the roles and you need to promote yourself to them.

In this chapter, I give you a plan for targeting agents and soliciting them for representation. Then I explain how to approach casting directors in an effective manner. Finally, I describe a cycle of mailings that will enable you to incorporate your audition search, your agent search, and your casting director search into an organized effort that will help you build contacts quickly and effectively.

UNDERSTANDING THE TALENT
AGENCY POWER STRUCTURE

When you're starting out, you can't be too picky about who your agent is. You always want to try to get the best agent possible, but as a beginner, it helps to remember that your first agent will probably be a stepping-stone to another agent, especially if you live outside of New York or Los Angeles. There are a group of agencies in Hollywood collectively known as "The Big Five." They are International Creative Management (ICM), Creative Artists Agency (CAA), the William Morris Agency, United Talent Agency (UTA), and Endeavor. There are other very powerful and well-respected agencies, but these five combine to represent the majority of the most powerful actors in the industry. Since you're a beginner, nobody at these agencies is going to talk to you. They won't take your phone calls and they won't return your letters. These agents work by referrals only. Your job is to work yourself into a position where somebody can refer you to a major agency.

Former William Morris agent and current talent manager Chris Fenton explains it this way: "It's all about networking. We have a network of people that we're in touch with that includes agents, casting directors, and production personnel. When we talk, they'll say, 'Hey, I just saw this actor audition and you should look at her,' or, 'I just saw this guy in a short film and he looks like someone you'd be interested in.' That's how we hear about people."

If you're brand-new to the business, then nobody's going to call a major talent agent and say, "Hey, I just saw this kid from New Hampshire walking down the street. He says he wants to be an actor so you should sign him." That's not going to happen. If, however, you get involved in a workshop, and you find auditions on your own, and you pursue all the avenues that are available to you, then you'll be able to get a lower-level agent who can start sending you out on better auditions in front of real casting directors. Without even realizing it, you'll immerse yourself in the very network of insiders that Chris Fenton just mentioned. These are the people who talk to bigger agents and casting directors. If you're good, people are going to talk about you and doors will open. That's the way you move up the ladder. It's now your job to contact the types of agents who are likely to talk to someone like you. Here's how you do it.

HOW TO CONTACT AGENTS

Contrary to popular belief, agents rarely "discover" actors. Actors get agents to represent them by asking. How you do this will vary depending on where you live, but I cover everything here so that you can pick the strategy that is right for you. I first explain how to target the right agent. Then I explain how to find contact information for each agent. Finally, I explain how to actually contact the agents. Later I do the same thing for casting directors, and you'll soon learn that there are similarities in how this is done. Before you begin actually contacting them, here are four points to consider:

1. Are you targeting the right type of agent?
2. Is the agent legitimate?
3. Is the agent in your area?
4. Does the agent accept unsolicited materials?

TARGET THE RIGHT AGENTS

It's important to know that different types of agents represent different types of talent. Agents can represent writers, producers, comedians, singers, actors, and more. Within the acting category, you need to be concerned with two common distinctions. These are "theatrical" and "commercial." Theatrical agents represent actors for movies and TV, which is often referred to as "MP/TV." If you say, "I'm looking for a theatrical agent," most in the business will understand what you're talking about. Commercial agents represent actors for commercials, which can be broken down further into "television" and "print." If an agent doesn't specialize, then he or she is called "full service." If you live in a small town, you don't have to be too concerned with this because there isn't as much work as there is in the big city. If you live in the big city, however, it's very important to know exactly what the agent represents.

It's not uncommon for an actor to have more than one agent. Some actors have an agent for commercials and another agent for theatrical work. When you meet with an agent, make sure you know exactly what you're being represented for and whether or not you can get a separate agent for other areas of work.

GET YOUR START IN COMMERCIALS

Beginners often have a much better chance of signing with a commercial talent agent, because commercials often require very specific types of looks, age, and abilities. Acting experience isn't always as important. Commercial casting directors feel the same way. If a casting director needs an actor with a very specific look or skill, she'll be less concerned with experience.

Have you ever noticed how many ads there are for senior citizens? Ads for medications, hospitals, insurance, and other items often require actors in their seventies and older. If you're a talent agent and you don't have any seventy-year-old actors, you'll be likely to meet with a seventy-year-old who sends you a headshot because you know there is work out there for that type, and you don't care too much what the actor's experience is.

Children and babies can also get their start in commercials because sometimes the job calls for a cute kid who can talk well and isn't shy. Experience, headshots, and résumés aren't as important as they are for film and TV actors. Erika Christensen, star of *Traffic* and *Swimfan,* got her start in a McDonald's commercial at age twelve.

Special skills are also something that can get you a role in a commercial. Think about all the ads that feature skateboarding, biking, skiing, and other extreme sports. If you can do one of these things well, you might find yourself in an ad. Imagine if Nike needs skydivers for their latest commercial. Your résumé has one play on it, but in your special skills section, you listed skydiving. Your agent will send you on the audition and he doesn't care if you can act.

Unique looks are also in high demand among commercial talent agents and casting directors. Today there's a high demand for an "edgy" look. This often means pierced body parts and other unique features. That doesn't mean that you should go out and pierce your tongue today. By the time you read this, those might not be the hip styles anymore. My point is that agents and casting directors are looking through headshots all week, and if something about your look makes them stop and say, "Wow," then you might have a chance to get called, and they won't necessarily care how much experience you have. Once you get signed with a commercial agent, then the doors can open up for other opportunities if you prove to be a good actor, so this is a good place to start.

IS THE AGENT LEGITIMATE?

An assumption used to be that if an agent was franchised by SAG, the agent was legitimate. Don't worry if you don't know what that means exactly. As I write this, the agreement between SAG and the talent agents has expired. Both organizations are working together in good faith, but their future is not clear. Agents who are working within the rules of SAG, even though they don't have a formal agreement with SAG, are now called "SAG compliant." Therefore, when you approach agents, ask them if they are SAG franchised or SAG compliant. If they say no to either, it doesn't necessarily mean they're not legitimate, but it's a sign that you need to ask more questions.

In smaller markets, agents aren't necessarily going to be SAG franchised because the volume of work doesn't support it. If an agency is listed in one of the professional publications like Ross Reports, then it's probably a legitimate agency, but always do your homework. The best resource is to ask your fellow actors.

The oldest rule in show business is that you should never pay an agent a fee. Rather, an agent gets paid a commission when she gets work for you. I receive a constant stream of e-mails from actors in small towns who ask about agent fees and tell me stories about how some agent wanted $500 or $1,200 up front. No legitimate agent will ask you for a fee. These fees often cover the costs of photos, websites, training, and anything else they can think of. It doesn't matter how they justify it. A legitimate agent will not ask you for a dime.

You might be thinking, "But Pete, if this guy said he can get me work, why do I care if he charges a fee?" If this guy is so confi-

Top publications for finding agents:

- *The Agencies* **(Acting World Books)**
- *The Right Agent* **(Silverscreen Publishing)**
- *Agents and Managers* **(ifilm Publishing)**
- *Ross Reports* **(VNU Business Publications)**

You can safely assume that if an agency is listed in these types of publications, it's legitimate.

dent about getting work for you, then why does he need to collect money up front? Agents who charge fees are considered scammers, and they should be avoided.

You also need to make sure that the agency is not some kind of school. I get e-mails all the time from actors who say, "Pete, I have an audition with an agency called the Sunshine Modeling Club of greater New Jersey." I e-mail them back and tell them they are not auditioning for an agency. They are auditioning for a school that has used some carefully crafted ads to trick aspiring actors into thinking that it is an agency.

If you can't figure out whether or not it's an agency, then it probably isn't. Ask an agent if you can speak with some of his other clients and ask the clients how they like working with this agent and what to expect. No legitimate agent will have a problem with such a request.

A legitimate agent will not insist that you take any classes from him or that you use a particular photographer. Agents can recommend photographers whom they know and trust, but if they insist that you use somebody, then you should walk away.

A legitimate agency is run by agents and assistant agents. There is usually one person or a few partners who own the agency, and they often have a name associated with the agency. For example, Abrams Artists, Berzon Talent, and Bobby Ball Talent are real agencies named after real people. Acme Talent is not named after a person, but it's a real agency, and you can find out the names of the agents if you ask. If the agency you're meeting with is run by a mysterious corporation, and you can't find the names of any actual agents, then you should be very careful. Legitimate agencies are not run by associates and sales reps who call actors anonymously and ask them to come in and "audition."

You can't be afraid to confront agents. Ask them point-blank if they are agents. Ask them how they get paid. If they say any-

If you aren't sure about an agency, call **SAG**. Go to its website, www.sag.org, and find the contact number for your area. **SAG** has real people who answer the phone and will gladly help actors. Another site to check is www.agentassociation.com. This is an organization of talent agents that also lists legitimate agents.

thing other than, "I get a percentage of the work that I book for you," then you should walk away. Use some sense and if you're not sure, bring a parent or friend and check out the agent together. The resources that I'm going to provide for you will steer you toward legitimate agents but you need to do your research. You can always call other agents or managers to ask about a particular agent. Most won't mind helping you avoid a scam.

In March 2002, I was approached by a literary agent who asked me if I'd be interested in writing a book about acting. I didn't know the agent, so I suspected that he was a salesman for some kind of self-publishing company where I'd pay to have my own book published. The first thing I did was visit his website, www.ventureliterary.com. I was pleasantly surprised to see that he was a real literary agent with real clients and a list of previously published books. I contacted the publishers that he worked with and was reassured that he was legitimate. Once I had confirmed all of that, I then contacted him and we talked. He eventually became my literary agent, and he is the guy who got me the deal to write this book. The point is: Do your homework.

Is the agent in your area and will he or she accept an unsolicited submission?

As I mentioned in the chapter on casting, agents simply can't waste their time working with people who don't live in their area. That doesn't mean they won't talk to someone who doesn't live in their area, but they won't work with an actor who doesn't live close by. It goes beyond logistics. Imagine you live in Arizona and you claimed you could get to Los Angeles within two hours at any time—even guaranteeing that you would never be late and you would always be available. Many actors claim they'll do that and that's impossible, but even if that were somehow true, the fact that you don't live in Los Angeles tells an agent that you're not completely dedicated to acting. If you were, you'd move to the city where acting jobs happen. Nothing is more important than your dedication. So stick to the agents in your area.

Some beginners don't know what an "unsolicited" submission is, and that's okay. You're not supposed to know everything. That's why you're reading this book. A tape or a letter sent to an agent even though that agent didn't ask for it is considered an unsolicited submission. The more powerful an agent or manager gets, the less likely she is to open an unsolicited package. There are legal concerns that are too complicated to explain and now there are even security concerns. The bottom line is that you have to find someone who'll actually open an unsolicited letter from you.

YOUR PLAN OF CONTACT

Now that you know what you're looking for, it's time to find an agent. Your goal is to find someone who'll meet with you and agree to represent you. If you're in a major market like Los Angeles or New York, you'll probably have better luck targeting commercial talent agents first. If you're in a small market, the agents will probably all be full service agents, so you'll just target any that you can find.

You'll begin by performing research and creating a list of the people you wish to contact. Next you'll begin contacting them. Last, you'll create a schedule to follow up with them.

FINDING THE AGENTS IN YOUR AREA

You can use several sources to find agents in your area. If you live in one of the major entertainment cities, I would suggest going to the Samuel French bookstore. Samuel French carries current publications that list agents along with contact information. On the Web you can get this information at the Academy Players website, www.acadpd.org. Another great source is www.hcdonline.com, which carries books of agents and managers. Also, the SAG website, www.sag.org, provides lists of agents. A publication generally carries more information about the agent. Many websites list only a name and contact information.

Here's an example of an agency listing found on the SAG site under "Hollywood" agents.

Dorfman, Craig S & Associates
6100 Wilshire Blvd., Suite 310
Los Angeles, CA 90048
Tel: (323) 937-8600
Type: (T-A)

This listing tells you the agency name, contact information, and the fact that the agency represents "theatrical" and "adults" (T-A). This is better than nothing, and it wouldn't hurt to send this agency a letter, but since you don't want to waste any time or money, it would help if you knew more about this agency.

For a more complete listing, I would suggest a book called *Agents and Managers* published by ifilm Publishing and available online at www.booksaboutacting.com. This publication lists agents and managers nationwide along with complete contact information and detailed lists of the type of talent they represent. This directory is heavily used in the industry. Here's a sample listing:

Dorfman & Associates, Craig

6100 Wilshire Blvd., Suite 310

Los Angeles, CA 90048

Tel: (323) 937-8600

Fax: (323) 937-7360

Represents: Actors, comedians, legitimate theater, young adults/teens

Craig Dorfman	Owner
Terri Kelly	Agent
Matthew Schooler	Asst.
Tyrone White	Asst.
Damyon Thomas	Asst.

This book obviously gives a lot more information. Now you know a little more about what type of actors are represented and how big the agency is. There are two agents and three assistants. That would be considered small to midsize. It's hard to judge whether or not the agency would be willing to work with a newcomer, but you could certainly add this to your list of prospects. It's also good to know the assistants because today's assistants are tomorrow's agents.

Here's a listing from a publication called *The Right Agent* from Silverscreen Publishing. This monthly publication is available at the Samuel French bookstore.

Dorfman & Associates, Craig

6100 Wilshire Blvd., Suite 310

Los Angeles, CA 90048

Tel: (323) 937-8600

Fax: (323) 937-7360

Craig Dorfman and Terri Kelly represent talent for Motion Pictures/TV. Represent adults, young adults 18 and over. Represents mostly established actors with very strong credits. New clients are mostly from industry referrals; however don't send tape unless requested.

Now you have a lot more information, and you just saved yourself the cost of mailing your headshot. This is not the type of agency that is looking for a beginning actor with few or no credits. That doesn't mean you can't try to contact them, but you should wait until you have more experience to solicit an agent like this. It should be very obvious to you how helpful it is to have information like this while searching for an agent.

Here's an entry from a book called *The Agencies,* published by Acting World Books.

Daniel Hoff Agency
1800 Highland Ave., Ste 300
Hollywood, CA 90028
323-962-6648

Daniel Hoff handles Commercials—is currently seeking African-American, Hispanic & Asian Talent, Young, Edgy, Alternative Talent 18–25, Dancers, Comedians, Moms, Dads, Seniors. Submit head shot and résumés by mail. Casting people say it's an excellent, hardworking, smart group.

Look at all that information. If you're a young Asian dancer, then it sounds like a good place to send your headshot. The more information you have, the better off you're going to be. A general list of agents isn't going to do you much good. Time spent doing research with a book like this will save you lots of time and money in the long run.

The *Agents and Managers* book lists agents from across the country. The other publications focus mainly on Hollywood and New York. If they don't list the agents near your city, I would suggest visiting the website of your local film commission. All U.S. states have a film commission, and many countries have similar organizations. The film commissions list movie-producing resources and usually include links to casting directors and agents in your state.

I just pulled up the site of the Oregon state film and video office, www.oregonfilm.org. After clicking on the "Production Directory" link, I found a list of items that I could search for. I chose "Talent Agencies" and found six listings for the state of Oregon. I clicked on one called Ryan Artists Inc. and found that it has a website. On its website I found out what kind of talent the agency is looking for and instructions for sending a headshot and résumé. If you're an actor in Oregon, you could send this agency your information.

If you don't want to use the Web or a book, you still have another option—networking. It's one of the cheapest and easiest ways to get what you want and is covered in step seven of Your Acting Plan. Go to your local theater and talk to the actors who are rehearsing there. Just walk in and introduce yourself. They'll be able to tell you about all the local agents, casting directors, and audition opportunities.

PREPARE YOUR TARGET LIST

Using the resources I just mentioned, make a list of all the agents you wish to contact. If you're using one of the publications, pick the agencies that are small to midsize and that will accept submissions from new talent. Make sure they're in your area. You might also consider targeting commercial agents, too, if there's something unique about you. Spend a day creating that list. If you live in Los Angeles or New York, you might come up with sixty agents. If you live in Kentucky, you might find three or four. Regardless of the number, make the list.

Once you have this list, you should study it a bit. Even though you're going to start by sending letters, it's helpful to learn the names of these agents. Imagine that you read a news story about an agent who'll be giving a seminar at some event. If that agent's on your list, the name should jump out at you and you should attend that event. You might meet another actor on a shoot who says, "I'm with so-and-so agency." If you recognize that agency, you might get an introduction. Knowledge will help you in your networking efforts, so absorb as much about the industry as possible.

TIME TO CONTACT THE AGENTS

Once you have your list, it's time to approach the agents. Avoid calling them. They don't like it, and they don't have time for it. However, if you only found a phone number, call the agent up and say, "Hello, I would like to know what your submission policy is for actors seeking representation." That's all you say. Don't tell them that you're a beginner or that you really want to be an actor, or that you were just wondering about something. Say that line clearly and confidently. If they say, "We don't see new talent," then you thank them and hang up. If they tell you that they see new talent on Thursdays at 3:00, then you ask them what you need to bring. Have a pen and paper handy to take notes. If you ask a short, professional question like that, they will not get angry. Don't keep them on the line. Just get your information and get off the phone. Whatever they tell you to do is what you'll do.

PREPARE YOUR COVER LETTER

Cover letters should be short and sweet. You're telling the agent that you're an actor and you want representation. You can also add a few brief items that might give the agent more information about your skills and training, but don't start pleading or trying to convince them that you're hardworking. They know what you want. Here's an example.

Peter Jazwinski
1313 Mockingbird Lane
Los Angeles, CA 90046
pete@myactingagent.com
h: 310-555-8890
c: 310-555-5432

July 31, 2002

Homer Davis
Bufont Talent Agency
Los Angeles, CA 90028

Dear Homer,

I'm currently studying acting at the Acting Naturally work-shop in Hollywood, and I'm seeking representation. I recently performed in the play *Picnic* at the Fritz Theater, and I'm flu-ent in three foreign languages: Russian, Polish, and French.

I am actively auditioning each week for independent film proj-ects and plays, and I'm booking roles regularly. I have enclosed a current headshot and résumé for your consideration. I'll gladly send you a VHS copy of my reel if you'd like. Please contact me when you're ready for someone of my type.

Sincerely,
Peter Jazwinski

You might not be fluent in three languages and you might not have a reel to show. If you don't know what a reel is, go back to step three, "The Basics." The very least you should write is "Hi, I'm seeking representation and I would like to meet with you." That's the minimum requirement.

Whatever you do, don't beg and plead and tell them how much you really want to be an actor and how it's always been your life's dream, and so on. Agents already know that. Your headshot and résumé are all they need to see. Agents don't have time to read long cover letters. Although they don't want to read your life's story, it helps if you can show them some passion and commitment. If you state that you're actively auditioning for projects on your own, and that you're studying regularly, then they'll know that you're serious and dedicated.

Don't worry about fancy fonts, exotic stationery, or laser copies. Any current home computer can print out a clean-looking letter on regular white paper. Buying fancy parchment or colored stationery is going to make you look like an amateur. It's also possible that you could send out hundreds of these, so you need to think about cost. Keep it clean, simple, and professional.

> This is just my opinion, but I always prefer a handwritten
> cover letter because it shows some thought. I can tell when
> I receive a form letter with my name inserted into it.
> —Scott-Arthur Allen,
> talent manager and acting coach

Write a cover letter for every agent to whom you're mailing. Address the agent personally. "Dear Meg" is fine, but "To whom it may concern" is not. It shows that you haven't done your research, and you don't know what you're talking about. If you don't know who the agent is, then don't write to that agency.

PREPARE THE ENVELOPES FOR THE MAIL

Use a standard 9 by 11 mailing envelope just like you used for your audition submissions. You can buy these in bulk at a local office supply store. You don't need padded envelopes or windows or anything else fancy. Enclose your headshot, résumé, and cover letter. Your résumé should be trimmed so that it's the same size as your headshot. Then staple your résumé to the back of your headshot using four staples. Most copy shops like Kinkos will cut your résumé for you so that you don't have to trim each one with scissors.

Do not send a video unless they ask for one. Make sure you put the agent's name on the envelope as well as the agency name. If you do this, it's more likely to go to the agent's desk. Take this to the post office and mail it. It's good to include a return address so that you can find out if any of your addresses are incorrect. Agents and agencies change often and sometimes it's hard to find the most up-to-date contact information.

TRACK THE SUBMISSIONS

You need to keep a record of who you're submitting to and when, just like you do for your audition submissions. Go back to your notebook and make a new tab called "Agents." Just add the agent's name and address along with the date that you sent your submission. It's likely that you'll be mailing to these agents again, so it's important to keep an organized record.

WHAT ABOUT LABELS?

Much has been made about address labels. Many services sell lists of preprinted address labels with the names of all the major talent agents on them. Some actors worry that these are too impersonal and that an agent will only open a letter if the address is handwritten. Agents don't care if you use labels or not. They're too busy to worry about that. Oftentimes the mail is opened by assistants anyway. As always, your headshot and résumé will do the talking.

Perhaps you're wondering if you should buy these address labels. They're certainly a good thing to have, but the problem is that you probably won't use them all. I once bought a pack of agency and casting director labels. Hundreds of agents were

Many agents and casting directors complain about large envelopes that are sealed up like Fort Knox. They have to open hundreds of letters a day, so make it as easy as possible. If the envelope has a clasp on it, just bend the clasp and don't seal the sticky part. Don't be paranoid. Mail carriers in Los Angeles aren't interested in looking at your headshot. They've seen them all.

listed, but I wasn't targeting all those agents, so most of them were wasted. I prefer to create my own through research and to update them as I go. Another problem with the agency labels is that they typically list the agency or the owner on the label. If you're contacting a specific agent in that agency, then the label is useless. They aren't too expensive, so it's not a complete waste if you buy a pack, but do your research first.

MAIL AGAIN IN TWO MONTHS

After you send your letter, do not call the agent to follow up! Agents don't like unsolicited phone calls. If they want you, they will call you. You are not going to be able to sell yourself on the phone. You will probably end up angering the agent. The agent is probably not going to call you, so don't expect a call the first day after you've done your mailings. Once you've mailed to an agent, you have to go back to step four and continue to look for auditions on your own. That's all you can do. If you don't hear from the agent, do another mailing in two months. Here are the reasons why:

- The timing could be wrong.
- Many agents won't consider talent that isn't referred by someone in the industry.
- You might not have enough credits on your résumé.
- The agent only works with union talent.

- Your headshot doesn't interest the agent.
- The agent already has one or more actors who are your type.
- You don't live in the same city as the agent.

A great deal of luck is involved in the business, and if it isn't with you, then your package could get lost or tossed out. If agents only work by referral, then they'll toss you out unless you drop someone's name. As you network and build contacts, you might meet an actor whom the agent represents or used to represent. If you put that person's name in your next cover letter, it just might buy you that extra second you need to get noticed.

> Mail your headshots to the same agents every two months because things might be completely different the next time they see your photo.
>
> —Sandra Merrill, talent agent
> and former casting director

If an agent tosses you out because you're too inexperienced, he might consider you two months later if you've acquired another credit or two. That's why it's important to continuously revisit step four to find more roles. If an agent only works with union talent, you might have a shot if you manage to get into the union in two months. If your headshot doesn't interest her, she might be in a different mood the next time or you might have a new headshot the next time you submit to her.

Maybe an agent likes you, but he already has an actor of your type and doesn't want to represent two of the same kind of actor. If you submit again in two months, that other actor may have moved on and now the agent does need your type. Last, if you didn't live in the same city as the agent, but now you do, you just might get a call. These are the many reasons why you need to resubmit in two months if you don't hear from an agent.

BE PERSISTENT BUT DON'T BE A NUISANCE

Many agents and casting directors admire persistence and like to reward it. However, it pays to know when to stop because you don't want to be a pest. Here's an e-mail I received from an actor in search of an agent.

> Pete,
>
> I met an agent while waiting at the airport, and after talking for a while, he said that I should send him my headshot and résumé. I mailed it to him the next day but didn't hear anything from him so I mailed him another one. I've left him two phone messages, but he hasn't called back. Do you think I should go to his office?

I told this woman to stay away. I wouldn't have called this agent twice. Two mailings is okay, but two phone calls is likely to get you banned. I can't stress enough that if agents want you, they'll call you. If she calls this guy one more time, he's more likely to take out a restraining order than he is to sign her.

I had an actor in my workshop who got an interview with an agent and was told to his face that she wasn't interested in signing him. Later he called the receptionist at the agency and asked him to put in a good word for him. He had already met the agent face-to-face. That's the best he can hope for. Take your shot and move on. Be persistent in your pursuit of agents, but don't badger them. The time you waste chasing agents who aren't interested could be better spent trying to find someone who *is* interested.

WHAT TO DO IF AN AGENT ACTUALLY
WANTS TO SEE YOU

If an agent calls and wishes to meet with you, try to gather some information first. Get the time and location and ask the agent what he wants you to bring. He might ask you to bring more headshots or your proof sheet in case he wants to choose a new headshot for you. You should present yourself in a manner that is similar to your headshot. Give agents what they like. If they ask you to meet after normal business hours or if they ask you to come to their home, be very careful. SAG rules state that SAG franchised agents can't work out of their homes.

As far as the actual interview is concerned, there isn't much I can tell you that's going to change how you present yourself. There are books written about this subject, but I don't think it really matters. You shouldn't need coaching on how to shake hands, how to dress, or how to speak. I could tell you not to be obnoxious or boring, but if you have to be reminded of that, then you don't have much of a chance. If you've gotten to that point on your own, then you should be able to close the deal. Think passion. Here are a few pointers that will help:

- Look agents in the eyes whenever you talk to them and speak from your heart.
- Ask them to explain the general points of your contract and ask them what they expect from you on a daily and weekly basis.
- Don't be afraid to say or do anything. Contrary to popular belief, what you say isn't all that important. It's your overall persona that is on display. Ask them anything you want, but ask something to show that you're alive. Mostly you'll be answering questions. It probably won't last long, so make the most of it.
- Don't sign anything in their office. No legitimate agent will rush you into anything. If you're not a lawyer, then take your contract to someone who can explain it to you.

WHAT SHOULD I LOOK FOR IN
AN AGENT CONTRACT?

Agent contracts aren't as standard as they used to be, and as I mentioned previously, you should take it to an independent party to have it explained. Here are some of the main items you should be concerned with:

1. **Length of contract**—This is typically one to three years.
2. **Percentage of commission**—For acting agents, 10 percent is a standard commission.
3. **Types of commission**—You need to find out what constitutes a commission. If you get a $500 plane ticket to go to the shooting location, does the agent take a percentage of that?
4. **How to break the contract**—Most contracts have clauses that state something to the effect that if the agent hasn't procured work for you in ninety consecutive days, then you can break the contract.

These are just a few of the many things that might be included in a contract. If you have any questions about anything in your contract, contact your local SAG office. You can get that contact info from their website, www.sag.org.

ASK SOME QUESTIONS

If you meet with an agent, you should prepare some questions to ask so that you're not just sitting there nodding with nothing to say. Agents aren't going to string you along for weeks wondering whether or not to sign you. If they call you in, it's because they want to work with you. If you look exactly like your headshot, and you come across as an interesting, creative person, they'll probably ask to work with you. Here are some questions that you should definitely include. You can ask more than this, but this is a good start.

1. What are your plans for me? Agents don't just sign people for no reason. It's okay to ask what they have in mind for you.

2. How often and how should I contact you?
3. How many headshots do you need from me to start with, and how will you communicate to me that you need more?
4. If I have an urgent matter that requires your assistance or knowledge, how should I contact you?
5. If I hear about an audition that I want to be submitted for, how should I contact you?
6. Is it okay for me to simply drop by the office at any given time?
7. Is there anything specifically that I should or shouldn't do on my own as far as looking for work is concerned?

Once you establish these guidelines with your agent, you'll both have a solid understanding of what's to be expected. Some agents will tell you never to drop by the office unexpectedly. Others won't mind at all. I know agents who conduct all business via fax. It depends on the agent, and it's up to you to establish your parameters on the first day. If you don't, you could be looking at a very stale relationship, and that's not fun or productive. I've known plenty of actors who signed with an agent, didn't ask them any questions, and then they never heard from the agent again. I know that sounds strange, but it happens. Don't let it happen to you. Go in with your questions prepared.

OTHER WAYS TO MEET AGENTS

Mailings are the most common and widely used method for contacting agents, but the most effective way to meet agents is through personal referrals. That doesn't mean that you have to have an agent as a neighbor, but it wouldn't hurt. Networking is extremely important in the entertainment business, and that's why I dedicate a chapter to it later. I got my first agent through a personal referral, so I want to take a moment here to address the subject.

While working as a tour guide in Hollywood, I met a young woman who worked part-time as an agent's assistant. We became friends and she saw me putting together my headshot and résumé during work breaks. She learned I was an actor and asked me if I needed an agent. She told her agent about me and arranged a meeting. I met the agent and got signed. It was that easy. Or was it?

I didn't get an agent just because I knew someone. I had a headshot, résumé, and training, and I was actively pursuing acting. I got that agent because the girl I worked with had grown to know me and liked me. She went to the agent and said something like, "I know this guy who's a pretty good actor and he has a good all-American look. I think he could get work. Would you like to meet him?" It turned out that the agent actually specialized in Hispanic talent. Therefore, she didn't have any clients with my kind of look. She was in a small agency and was willing to take a nonunion actor because her trusted assistant vouched for me. It's very possible that an agent like that could receive a picture from a guy like me and say, "Nah, not my type." However, because her assistant said I was a good guy and a good actor, her whole perception of me changed.

Here's another example of how a referral can work. Imagine you've been following the steps of Your Acting Plan and you land an audition in front of a casting director for a film or TV show. You don't get the part, but the casting director tells you that she really liked your performance. She said you're a good

If you want an immediate response from an agent, enclose a stamped postcard addressed to you. Write these two sentences: (1) Yes, I would like to meet with you, I'll call you, and (2) No, I'm not interested at this time. Try again in two months. Include a checkbox next to each sentence, and you'll have your answer in no time.

actor, but you just weren't right for the part. If they're impressed enough, they might say that. If that happens, you can ask that casting director for a referral. If she was sincere, she'll want to help you get an agent, and she'll be able to give you plenty of names to call. The recommendation of a casting director is a sure foot into the door of an agency.

Many actors in Los Angeles choose the best-known acting teachers and acting classes because of the possible referrals. If you're studying with someone who is considered a top teacher, then putting that on your résumé might open a door. Agents and casting directors know who the best teachers are, and they are often friends with them. Friends talk. Of course, this will only help you if you're a good actor. You can't just sign up with a top teacher and think that you'll get discovered. You have to deliver the goods.

HOW TO CONTACT AGENTS FROM OUT OF TOWN

As you already know by now, you shouldn't waste an agent's time if you don't live in the same city. Agents don't want to work with out-of-towners, but they'll gladly talk to you if they like you. Here's what you do. Send the same cover letter we've already discussed, but include this line somewhere. "I'm moving to (their city) in two months and I would like to meet with you when I arrive."

An agent will have no problem with that. If he doesn't want to meet with you, you'll never hear from him again. If he likes you and wants to meet, then he'll let you know. If that happens, then you have to deliver your promise of moving. Don't be late.

ACTION POINTS FOR CONTACTING AGENTS

- Before approaching an agent, build some experience so that you have something to offer, and make sure you have all the basics covered, including the best headshot you can afford.

- When you're ready to approach an agent, use a good reference guide to target the right ones.
- Establish a regular cycle of letter writing and networking to reach agents.
- While you're trying to reach agents, keep looking for work on your own so that you can build the résumé and experience.

Part 2: Contacting Casting Directors

Now that you know how to submit to agents, it's time to turn your attention toward contacting casting directors. Casting directors are the people who actually cast movies, TV shows, theater, and commercials. As I explained in the chapter on the casting process, these are the people whom you ultimately want to meet. Nearly everything I've said about contacting agents applies to contacting casting directors, too. You have to present yourself professionally, and you have to approach the casting directors in your area who are looking for your type. The best way to meet a casting director is to have an agent, but since you don't have an agent yet, you should submit on your own.

There are two goals for contacting casting directors. The first, of course, is to get called in for an audition. They might call you in specifically for something that they're auditioning at that time, or they might call you in for a general interview, which is also known as a "general." During a general, they just want to meet you and see what you're like in person. That way they'll have a better idea of your look and personality when it's time to cast something. Both such meetings are excellent opportunities for you.

The second goal is to simply build familiarity with casting directors. They are very busy people who receive letters and photos every day, and they can't possibly keep track of every actor they saw once. If you can find a way to make them think about you on a regular basis, then they'll be more likely to call when they have something for your type. To accomplish these goals, you're again going to use a combination of letter writing and networking.

KNOW YOUR AUDIENCE

Just like with agents, you want to target the casting directors who are in your area and who would be interested in your type. To do this, you have to know what type you are. If you're a pretty, young woman from North Carolina, you could target the casting director of *Dawson's Creek*. That show films in North Carolina, and it's filled with pretty, young people. If you are a forty-something actor in Los Angeles, you could submit to the casting director of *The Agency* or *The West Wing*. They film in Los Angeles, and they often use those types. If you are an Italian from the New York area, you could submit to the casting director of *The Sopranos*. If you're an unusual-looking person or someone with an extraordinary skill, then you would especially target those who cast commercials. If you have exceptional training and a solid résumé, you could target those who cast features.

TARGETING CASTING DIRECTORS

In New York or Los Angeles, it's very easy to find lists of casting directors. The Samuel French bookstores carry them. You can also buy them online from www.breakdownservices.com. They sell a book called *C/D Directory* for New York and Los Angeles. These publications and others like them will list very specific information about casting directors. The Academy Players Directory website, www.acadpd.org, lists casting directors, but it will be a simple list without much detailed information. You want something that tells you what casting directors do and where they work so that you can target them effectively.

Don't ever explain yourself to a casting director. They don't want to know why you're late, whether or not you're feeling well, or how you feel about the character. They want you to come in and audition. Let your performance do the talking.

In addition to locating the casting directors, you need to find out what kinds of projects they cast. If you buy one of these directories, you'll see some of the following terms.

- Episodic—This means they cast for television series or "episodes." Usually they'll list the actual show that they cast.

- MOW—Movie of the Week. Ever see those Sunday night movies about the husband who was a spy or the teacher who slept with her student? Those are MOWs.

- Feature—This means they cast feature films like *Gangs of New York* and *Titanic*.

- Commercials—This means that they cast commercials.

- Pilots—These are the proposed television shows that are made each winter.

- Industrials—These are usually training films like you've seen at work or in school, something like *How to Use a Table Saw*.

These are the various categories you'll see, and these are typically for the big markets. All you need to concern yourself with are commercials, television shows, and features. Those are the main categories. Those who cast features are going to be hardest to meet because they rarely cast beginners, but that doesn't mean you can't contact them. It just means that your odds of connecting with them are very small, so it's best to look at commercials and television.

An entry from one of these directories will look something like this:

Janet Gilmore—Janet Gilmore/Megan McConnell
Episodic
Address
Phone
Project type: MOW, *The Practice,* Pilots

This means that Janet Gilmore is the casting director and the company name is Janet Gilmore/Megan McConnell. They cast movies of the week, pilots, and for the television show *The Practice.* If you want to send your headshot, the address is provided.

Commercial casting directors need new talent every day, and oftentimes they need a very specific look. The look becomes more important than acting abilities, and therefore your photo becomes more important than your résumé. Getting your photo in front of a commercial casting director is very important if you're just starting out. Some actors who got their start in commercials include Jason Biggs, Tara Reid, and Haley Joel Osment.

Television casting directors also need new talent every week, and they often need a certain look as well. By learning about specific TV shows and the casting directors who cast them, you can increase your chances of getting an audition.

If you live in a small market, there aren't going to be a lot of casting directors to choose from so it's unlikely that you'll find them listed in a book. In the small markets you'd be better served by talking to agents and actors in your area. On the Net you can look through your state's film commission website, just like you did when looking for agents. Also check any regional acting websites. Don't be discouraged about being in a small market and only having a few casting directors to work with. Even though there are less, the upside is that if you can impress one, you'll be considered for most of the work in that area.

The Ross Reports are pocket-sized reference books that list casting directors for Los Angeles, San Diego, and New York. They currently cost about $8 at Samuel French, and they're loaded with great info.

MAKE YOUR LIST

Using the resources listed, make a list of forty commercial casting directors and twenty TV casting directors to whom you're going to mail. If you're in a small market, make a list of any casting directors. These aren't rules, they're just examples. Keep in mind that you need to target those who are likely to use your type. Once you have this list together, get yourself on a schedule to do regular mailings. It's too time-consuming to mail to all of them at once, so pick out a number that will allow you to complete all your mailings in two months.

For example, if you found ten casting directors for your list, you could mail to all ten of them every two months, or you could mail to two or three of them each week. After eight weeks, you will have mailed to all ten. You want to mail to your list every two months just like you did for agents. This will breed familiarity, and you just might start to get noticed. I talk more about that at the end of the chapter when I discuss the mailing cycle.

MAILING TO A CASTING DIRECTOR

Mailing to a casting director is similar to an agent mailing. You include a headshot, résumé, and cover letter. Only the cover letter is going to change. Here's a sample cover letter that you can use:

Dear Mark:

I'm currently training at the Acting Naturally workshop in Hollywood, and I'd like to meet with you for a general interview. I've enclosed a headshot and résumé for your perusal. I'm auditioning for independent film projects and theater around town, and I'm actively seeking representation. Much continued success on (name of the show that they cast) and I look forward to meeting with you.

Sincerely,
Dave Hargreaves

That's all you need to include. Once again, don't let temptation cause you to add a bunch of nonsense about how you've always wanted to be an actor or how you'd be perfect for a particular role. The casting director will look at your photo and résumé and decide what to do with you. And please don't ever start any letter with "Hi, my name is . . ." It's just silly.

Casting directors much prefer that you know what you're submitting for. So if you don't know that a casting director is casting something specific, then you should request a general interview. If the casting director doesn't cast a TV show, then obviously you leave that part out. If you're currently appearing in something like a play, movie, or commercial, it would be very good to mention that. Casting directors and their assistants go to plays regularly and welcome theater invitations. It's the best way for them to judge your abilities.

When you're mailing to commercial casting directors, you should try to emphasize something about your special abilities. Remember, for commercials, looks and special abilities can sometimes outweigh acting experience. For example, if you can speak with different accents or if you can ride a unicycle or juggle flaming torches, you could mention that to a commercial casting director because that's a very specific skill that would put you on the short list if that particular need ever arises. You don't need to list your abilities in your letter if you already have them on your résumé, but if there's something particularly unique about you, you could mention it.

When mailing to TV casting directors, keep in mind that the most realistic expectation is to get a guest role or extra work. It's unlikely that a casting director will receive your picture and say, "Oh, yes, let's make him a new costar."

DOES MAILING TO CASTING DIRECTORS
REALLY DO ANY GOOD?

You might be very skeptical about mailing to casting directors. For many people, the idea of mailing a photo to the casting director of a hit television show seems like a waste. Why would they cast an unknown like you when there are so many experienced actors out there with agents getting regular auditions? That's a good question. Remember that this isn't something you're going to do for your entire career, but as a beginner you have to do everything possible to give yourself a chance to catch a break.

By submitting yourself to casting directors, you're exposing yourself and giving yourself an opportunity to be seen. Read what these casting directors have to say about submitting your headshot and résumé.

> I know there are many actors in this town (Los Angeles) who will tell you that they have been in this office and have been hired by sending a postcard or sending a picture and a résumé in the mail. No agent. No nothing.
> —Debra Zane, casting director
> for the Oscar-winning films *Traffic*
> and *American Beauty*

The best casting directors are going to visit the best theaters. Find out where the good theaters are and start looking for the auditions in those places. I've had students invite agents and casting directors to theaters that are an hour outside of Los Angeles on a weeknight. No agent is going to make that trip to see you in a small play.

I get 350 unsolicited head shots per week. I do open every piece of mail I get. I look at them all, and if someone is right for something I'm casting, or something innately interesting jumps out at me and I want to meet that actor, I will put that picture aside.

—Mark Teschner, casting director for
the soap opera *General Hospital*

Here are two industry professionals telling you that it is not a waste of time to mail your headshots to casting directors. Both of their names and addresses can be found by using the resources I listed earlier in this section. If that doesn't inspire you, I don't know what will.

For those of you in the smaller markets, here's something I found on the Oregon state film commission website, www.oregonfilm.org. I clicked on "Casting Directors" and found eight casting companies listed. I clicked the first one called Danny Stoltz Casting and read this information on their auditions page:

While we always recommend that actors, after learning about the business and perfecting their craft, seek representation from a reputable talent agency, there are still many opportunities for new and unrepresented actors. Not every project we cast requires professional actors; often, we are looking for "real people" of all types.

This casting director agrees with the steps of Your Acting Plan because he urges you to learn how to act and to get an agent, yet he's willing to work with beginners. This is the kind of information you need to know. If I were acting in Oregon, I'd send a headshot and résumé to this casting director immediately.

TRACK YOUR SUBMISSIONS

Time to open that notebook again and add another tab that says, "Casting Directors." You should add the name, address, date, and project that you submitted for. As time goes on, you'll develop a big list of contacts. You'll be mailing to these people again, so keep it organized.

THE MAILING CYCLE

In the previous chapter I covered audition mailings. Now I've covered agent and casting director mailings. It's time to put them all together to begin the mailing cycle. You're going to start a campaign of mailings that will help you find roles to build your résumé as well as recognition among agents and casting directors. If you stick with it, your chances of getting an agent and getting auditions will increase dramatically. Here's how you do it.

Choose two days of the week and take two to four hours on each day to do your research and mailings. On day one you'll go through all your casting sources. This will include the sources listed in the previous chapter. If you're using *Backstage,* then you should do this on Thursday. Set yourself a limit. If you find ten casting opportunities, then send out ten headshots, cover letters, and résumés to those ten notices. Write them down in your notebook each week so you know to whom you submitted and when.

On day two you're going to do your agent and casting director mailings. Once you have your lists compiled, choose a number that will allow you to mail to each person every two months as mentioned previously. You have to divide it up. Therefore, if you have a total of a hundred agents and casting directors to whom you're mailing, you'll have to mail to about twelve of them each week. That way they each get a photo from you every two months. There are obvious costs involved in doing this, and you're now learning what kinds of expenses are involved in being an actor.

If you're mailing to twelve agents and casting directors along with ten audition notices each week, that's twenty-two submissions. When you factor in the cost of your headshot, résumé, cover letter, envelope, and postage, you're at about 80 cents per mailing. That means you're close to $20 per week or $80 per month. That's something to consider in your budget when you think about becoming an actor.

WHY NOT DO ALL ONE HUNDRED MAILINGS AT A TIME?

You could do a hundred mailings all in one shot, but I don't recommend it. Imagine if you put a major typo like a wrong phone number on your résumé. You'd have to redo all hundred letters. Suppose you meet with an agent or casting director who tells you that your headshot doesn't look like you at all or that it is terrible. You might want to redo it. It's also very time-consuming and expensive to do a hundred mailings in one week. One of the main reasons, though, is that probably nothing will happen.

"Hey, Pete. Why are you telling me to do this if nothing's going to happen?" Great question. I can't tell you enough times that success in acting is often a matter of persistence. Think of your first mailing as your first step up Mount Everest. It doesn't seem like you've done anything, but you have to do it in order to get to the top.

Maybe the first mailing to an agent or casting director goes unnoticed. Remember how I mentioned that you could fall through the cracks, not be the right type, not be experienced enough, and so on? That first mailing didn't get you anywhere, but it laid the foundation for the next mailing.

If you're going to pick a regular day to do mailings, see if you can find another actor to meet with. You might be able to divide up tasks of printing letters and stuffing envelopes. It's also a way to support and motivate each other.

I met a TV producer who once told me that he and his partners had an unwritten rule that if they saw a person three times, they tried to cast them for something. He said that they always wanted to reward actors who were persistent.

You can't just walk up to agents and casting directors and say, "Hi, I'm hardworking and talented. Please hire me." Actually, you can do this but it's hard to find them outside of their offices. Your job is to make an impression on a casting director or agent. Persistence is one of the ways you can do that.

You'll recall when I discussed the casting process that agents and casting directors are constantly looking at photos. If your actual photo or résumé didn't make an impression because of outstanding looks or credits, then a onetime mailing isn't going to make an impression.

Imagine that your headshot and résumé come across the desk of one of these people every two months. They are going to start to remember you. They're going to think, "Hmm, there's that actor again. He sends me a headshot and résumé every other month. He sure seems determined. I'm going to see if I can find something for him." Now you've made an impression. It's still no guarantee of anything, but at least you're on their mind.

Weekly mailings help you establish a regular schedule of work. Los Angeles is filled with thousands of "actors" who came out here, got some headshots done, mailed them to a few or maybe even a hundred agents, and then did nothing. They sat around and waited to become famous. They never heard from

Think of your acting career as a smoldering coal that needs to be fanned constantly in order that it might burst into a flame. The mailings that you do to agents, casting directors, and to auditions are what keep the coals of your career glowing. If you stop doing these things, your career will go up in a puff of smoke.

the agents, so they gave up. Don't let that happen to you. If it were easy, everyone would have an agent. Also, if you miss one week due to illness or travel, you can get right back into it the following week. If you do one mailing every month or two, it's easy to keep putting it off. Routine helps you avoid procrastination.

By looking at the names of agents and casting directors every week, you'll also begin to learn their names, and that will help your networking efforts later. You'll also start to gain a sense of excitement because you'll become much more knowledgeable and enthusiastic about your chances. As your notebook of contacts grows, your chances of success will grow as well.

I run a networking group in Hollywood where I have actors actually come to my office and go through this routine each week. They meet, they print their letters, they make lists of agents, and they mail headshots and résumés. It takes them about two to three hours each session. At the end of the meeting, they say, "Wow, now I realize how much work it takes to get an agent." They also comment about how great they feel because they're working so hard. They're actually *doing* something—and they're sharing their experiences with other actors who are in the same boat as them.

THE SECOND ROUND OF MAILINGS IS
NOT THE SAME AS THE FIRST

You've been looking for auditions and mailing headshots to agents and casting directors for two months. Now it's time for your second round of mailings. Follow the same steps that you did in the first round but include these new ideas.

More research. Go back to your agent and casting directors list and find the first group you mailed to. You're going to mail to these people again. You should check to make sure they still exist. You could call them and ask to verify the name and address, but don't ask them anything else like, "Hi, did you get my photo last time?" Don't give them a chance to dislike you. Just get your information and get off the phone. Also, if any of your mailings came back with wrong addresses, find the new addresses or drop them from your list.

Once you confirm your list, it's time for the second round. By this time, you will have gone through at least a hundred head-shots. Now you see why you need to print about two hundred at a time. The second time you mail to an agent, it would be best to improve your résumé in some manner. Hopefully you've booked a play or taken a class or appeared in some kind of film or video since your last mailing. If you got a new credit since your last mailing, add that to your résumé and mention it in your cover letter. If it's a significant credit, you could enter it into your cover letter by saying something like, "I just wrapped production on the USC graduate film called *My Friend Grillo,* and I'm seeking representation."

During the second mailing to casting directors, you don't need a complete headshot, cover letter, and résumé. It won't hurt, but it can get expensive and there's an easier alternative. It's called "the postcard."

A postcard is a picture of your headshot printed on cardstock that is the same size as a standard postcard. I mentioned this in chapter 6 on the basics, and this is where it comes into play. It will have your name and phone number on it. I have examples of these on my website. The same shop that printed your head-shots will print postcards as well. Most places have deals where they'll give you two hundred postcards at a reduced rate if you order two hundred to three hundred headshots at the same time. It's a commonly used item.

The postcard doesn't include your résumé. It just has your name and contact number on the front. On the back it has room to write the address of the person you're sending it to along with a brief note. These are great for the second round of mailings to casting directors because they're so cheap.

Some agents warn against putting any personal information on your headshot or résumé. No home phone, no home address, and no social security number. If you have an agent, you put the agent's contact info. Otherwise, list your P.O. box and answering service phone number.

When you're mailing to a casting director for the second time, just send her a postcard. You can write a one- or two-sentence note on the postcard if you wish, but don't beg or try to sell yourself too hard. Regardless of what you write on it, what it "says" to the casting director is *I'm serious and persistent. Here's my photo again.* If it's a new photo, you could write something like, "Same great actor, brand-new photo for your records." The point is to keep it light and brief.

When mailing to the agents for a second time, you need to send the whole package. The agent should get a cover letter and résumé because you're making a formal request for representation. If you just send a postcard, then the agent doesn't necessarily know why you're sending it.

THE CYCLE SUMMARY

Let's review the cycle:

1. Make a master list of agents and casting directors in your area based on the guidelines listed. Do enough mailings each week to contact all your targets over the course of two months.
2. Pick one day each week when you mail to agents and casting directors. Pick another day of the week to do your audition mailings. After you do your mailings, print out that week's list and put it in your notebook so you can refer to it if you get a call.

3. Between mailings, search for other auditions and acting opportunities that don't require mailings. Continue your research for possible agents and casting directors to target.

4. After your first two months of mailings, you need to assess your situation. Do you need a new headshot? Is your résumé current? Are you targeting the right people?

5. Start the second round of mailings and include any changes made as a result of point four. For the second round of casting director mailings, just mail a postcard.

WHAT IF NOTHING HAPPENS?

If you try the cycle of mailings/looking for auditions/mailings/looking for auditions, and you don't give up, then the chances are very good that you'll get an agent. If you do one mailing and then forget about it, the chances are not that good. You have to stick with it.

Remember that "talent" is your ability to put yourself in a position to succeed. "Talent" is the ability to keep going when things get difficult. If you actually do two hundred mailings and don't get any responses, that is when you'll find out how badly you want to become an actor. If you want it very badly, then you won't even count the number of mailings.

Here are two e-mails that I received from actors with whom I've consulted through my website. See what you can learn from these examples.

Pete,

I am a talented young twenty-five-year-old New York actor who's been acting for twelve years. I have enough legit credits to fill two pages. Why can't I obtain an agent? Most of my credits are lead and supporting roles on TV/Film and Theater. I am a SAG and AFTRA member. I submitted headshots to sixty-five agents in two months and I only received one response for an interview, and that didn't work out because the agent wanted cash up front. Is there something I'm doing wrong?

Thanks,
Damian

What is wrong with Damian's plan? It sounds like he's doing pretty well, but he's missing a few things. First, it sounds like he only did one mailing. He said he did all sixty-five mailings in two months. Maybe those sixty-five headshots all fell off the mail truck. It's not likely, but that's another reason why I don't recommend doing them all at once.

He also mentioned that the one response he did get was from an agent who wanted to charge him money. Real agents don't charge money, so I wonder what kind of research he did. It's possible that he just got a list of agents somewhere and mailed them all without checking closely. If that's the case, he might also have mailed to agents who represent writers, producers, or children. If everything else he says is legitimate, then all he'll have to do is improve his research a bit and keep mailing each month. With his credits, I have no doubt that he'll get an agent soon.

Here's another e-mail that shows a different perspective:

Dear Pete,

I just wanted to tell you how grateful I am because my ten-year-old son signed with an agent today. I took your advice and researched all the child agents in Las Vegas. I sent his headshot out and got a call within two days. The agent said he needed someone exactly like my son and wanted to know if he was available for an audition that day. In just two days, my son had an agent and an audition. Thanks again.

Yours,
Veronica

You might think that Veronica just got lucky, but I don't see it that way. Luck is when you walk down the street and an agent spots you and says, "Hey, have you ever thought about being an actor?" What happened to Veronica and her son happened because she followed the steps of the plan and gave her son a chance to succeed. That's what you have to do.

ACTION POINTS

- Contacting agents and casting directors requires research.
- Dedicate a regular amount of time and money to contact these people.
- Your persistence and determination will be tested as you work the cycle of mailings.
- Utilize all the steps of the plan to contribute to your success.

DAILY GOALS

By now you should have a good idea about what agents and casting directors are looking for. If you're ready for this step, begin building a list of agents and casting directors whom you would like to contact. Pick one day on your calendar to do all your research, and pick another day to write your letters and do your mailings. Once you've done your research, pick a day on the calendar to do your first mailing. Stick to a regular schedule.

If you live in Los Angeles or New York, you should be able to create a list of sixty agents and forty casting directors very easily using the publications available. If you live in a smaller town, your list won't be as long, but that means you'll have less work to do. You should be excited because you're now starting the process of telling important people that you're an actor for hire. That's an exciting answer to the question "What did you do today to advance your acting career?"

9

STEP SIX: WORKING WITH AGENTS AND MANAGERS ON YOUR CAREER

By now you should be entrenched in the cycle of steps two, four, and five. That is, you're studying acting somewhere, you're looking for auditions on your own, and you're contacting agents and casting directors. Accomplishing all of this won't happen in the first month. Some actors stay in this cycle for years. That's okay, because you can get a lot done in this cycle. It's important to realize that two pitfalls are associated with this stage of your career. The first is that you could be tempted to give up because you can't get an agent. The second is that you stop working hard because you landed an agent and now you think everything will come to you. Knowing what to do at this stage will help you get to a higher level.

If you're feeling overwhelmed at this point, just take a breath. I'm not going to tell you to go out and get a manager just yet, especially if you just got an agent. I'm going to talk about your relationship with your agent first. The reason I mention managers at this point is that their duties are often confused with those of agents. In addition, if you're going to hire a manager, this is a good time. By the end of this chapter you'll know exactly how agents and managers work together, and you'll know whether you need to think about hiring a manager.

What agents and managers do

For many beginners it's confusing to understand the difference between agents and managers because they appear to do similar jobs. Part of the reason for this misconception is that there are so many questionable people, usually in small markets, who call themselves agents or managers when in fact they are nothing but salespeople trying to get your money. The differences between real agents and real managers are very distinct. Here's a quick breakdown.

Agents
1. Procure employment for the actor.
2. Interact with casting directors on behalf of the actor.
3. Negotiate contracts for the actor.
4. Take a 10 percent commission from the actor.

Managers
1. Help find an agent.
2. Act as liaison between actor and agent.
3. Might interact with a casting director on behalf of the actor.
4. Help organize the actor's personal and business needs.
5. Provide general show business education.
6. Guide the actor's career, including project development and publicity.
7. Take a 15 percent commission from the actor.

These are just general categories of course, but they should be enough to give you some idea about what each person does.

The agent sells the image that the personal manager creates.
—Lola H. Black,
Los Angeles talent manager

An agent finds jobs for you, while a manager finds a career for you

Agents spend most of their time on the phone talking with casting directors, producers, and other agents. They receive casting notices, and they send out the headshots and résumés of their actors. After one of their actors auditions, they'll usually talk to the actor and then possibly the casting director to see how it went. They will expect that you've completed the basics, that you know how to act, and that you're professionally organized and prepared. They won't help you with that. You either have to do it on your own or you can hire a manager to help you.

An agent might have twenty or a hundred actors that she represents. She can barely keep up with all the calls and submissions. She doesn't have time to ask you how your cat is. An agent won't help you get a good headshot, he'll just expect you to have one. Agents won't help you get a work permit if you're not a citizen, they'll just expect that you're able to work in the United States. Those are duties that a good manager can help you with.

For these reasons, agents are reluctant to work with new talent unless the talent is exceptional. An agent doesn't have the time or resources to educate you and teach you about the business. An agent wants you to make money for her so you have to be ready to go. This doesn't mean that agents are heartless or that they won't help you in any way. I simply want you to understand that because of the nature of their jobs, agents can't spend a lot of time helping you along. They'll look for work for you, but they'll expect you to be good enough and prepared

SCAM ALERT!

Be wary of the manager who tries to sell you classes, photos, or any other services. Managers will help you find classes and photographers, but if they are profiting directly from that venture, then they have a conflict of interest and they might be scamming you.

enough to book the work so that they can negotiate your contract and get their percentage.

A manager works with fewer clients and can therefore give much more personalized attention. Managers do not look for work for you. Instead, they look for the people who can help you get work, and they help prepare you to become a better actor. The manager can act as the go-between for you and your agent. That way you are free to concentrate on acting and you don't have to worry about politics and administrative matters. A good manager will also educate you so that you'll know what to expect at interviews and auditions.

A manager can help you organize your finances and ensure that you get to auditions on time, that you have a hotel room, and that you're treated fairly on the set. If you already have an agent, a manager can help you find a better one or can at least work with your current agent to make sure you're getting the best possible treatment. If you don't have an agent, a manager can help put together your whole team.

Managers can call the casting directors they know, and they can even introduce you to producers and filmmakers they know. Managers can help you find a good photographer and a good acting teacher. Once you're working as an actor, a manager can help find scripts and develop projects specifically for you. When you're ready for a publicist or a lawyer, a manager can assist you with those functions as well. In short, a manager does numerous hands-on activities to groom you, to promote your career, and to assist you in your personal and business life. That's how managers justify their higher percentage.

Managers are more likely to work with a beginner if they see potential simply because they have time. Some actually prefer to help you find a coach, find a photographer, and find an agent. They feel better about your chances since they're putting together the plan. In fact, most managers become managers for this very reason.

Neither agents nor managers charge fees

As I've already mentioned, agents and managers collect a percentage of your salary. That is, if you book a job, they take a percentage of the pay. If you make $1,000 on a film shoot, then the agent gets $100 (10 percent) and the manager gets $150 (15 percent). The remaining $900 or $850 goes to you. That's how it works with legitimate agents and managers. By the way, these percentages are not law, they are simply the industry standards.

There are countless managers who will take you on if you pay them a fee. They might say that the fee goes toward postage or photos or phone calls or anything else they can think of. Even though they're not breaking the law, the industry motto is "Never pay an agent or manager a fee." Most modeling schools are notorious for this kind of behavior. If a manager asks for any kind of upfront fees, just walk away, because he's probably not a good manager.

Now that you understand the agent/manager relationship, I want to address how you can promote your career at this point in Your Acting Plan. It's possible that you're still looking for an agent or manager. It's also possible that you could have one or both at this point as well. Regardless of your situation, once you get to this point there are still things you can do to get to a higher level. If you have an agent or manager, they can assist you in this effort.

You're not the agent's only client

If you have an agent at this point, or if you're close to signing with one, you have to remember that you might be one of fifty actors your agent represents. Even though she wants you and likes you, you're not the first thing on her mind each day. She already has actors who are working and making money for her, and she needs to give them the highest priority.

Also keep in mind that it takes time for casting directors to develop an understanding of who represents whom. The whole industry is built on a network of friendships, and it will take a while for your name and face to circulate and get known. That's assuming that your agent has connections. Because you're a beginner there's a good chance that the agent who signed you is not very powerful and doesn't have a lot of connections to begin with. Otherwise she wouldn't be signing beginners. She hears about auditions through the breakdowns, but she doesn't hear about *everything*. No agent hears about *everything*. This is yet another point where your persistence is going to be tested.

Establish a relationship with your agent

It might sound silly because your agent signed you and he must know you, but you'd be surprised how many actors don't have much of a relationship with their agents. I know plenty of actors who don't even get along with their agents and don't talk to them. They either talk to the assistant or they have a manager talk to the agent.

If you haven't talked to your agent in months, then you need to meet to discuss the situation. There's no reason for an agent to keep a client whom she doesn't send out on auditions. That's a losing situation for everyone.

Your relationship with your agent won't necessarily involve Saturday night dinners or even Wednesday morning phone conversations. What it involves is setting the ground rules of conduct so that you know what's expected of you. Make sure that when you leave the agent's office after getting signed, you know exactly what you're supposed to do on a daily basis. If you don't establish that, you might not ever see your agent again, and you might not ever talk to him again. Here's a quote from a working actor who asked me not to mention his name:

> My commercial agents and I have a tremendous relationship. I come in and say hello whenever I want. I do not communicate with my theatrical agents at all. I communicate with my managers, because my agents don't have time. This has led to a very stale relationship with my agents, however, so I think it was the wrong choice. My rule of thumb is that friends work harder for each other, so I want to befriend my representation as much as possible. It's a slow process, but once you have put in the time, you're in.

A "stale relationship" with an agent is something that happens to many actors who don't know what's expected of them or don't establish the rules up front. When it happens, it causes actors to think that their agents don't care or that the agents aren't any good. That's rarely the case.

When I signed with my first agent, I sat around for two months waiting for the phone to ring. It never did. I went to the agent's office to talk to her about it and when she saw me walk in she said, "Hey, Pete. How are you? Boy, am I glad to see you. I just got a call for a commercial audition for some fitness product. It's at 2:00 today. Can you make it?"

Of course I went to the audition, but before I did, she sat with me for about five minutes. She asked me what I was doing for myself. I was confused. I thought, "You're the agent. You're supposed to do everything." We never really got to talk about it completely because during my five minutes with her, her phone rang every thirty seconds. She was chatting up everyone who called and talked about auditions and interviews that involved her many clients. That's when I realized that just having an agent doesn't do much for you right away.

Before leaving my agent's office, I stopped to say hi to the assistants, but they were just as busy. They were stuffing envelopes with headshots to mail out while they were also opening envelopes from actors seeking representation. They were answering phones and gossiping while they worked very hard. They told me that they were out of my headshots and résumés and that they wanted me to bring a hundred more as soon as I could. Why didn't they tell me this before? Would they ever have told me if I hadn't walked in that day?

That's not an uncommon scene in a Los Angeles talent agency. Therefore, when you're starting out, don't expect your agent to do much more than mail your picture out, because when you're an unknown actor, that's about all they're going to do. That's still a great thing, because they're going to hear about a lot of auditions that you are never going to find anywhere, but you're still going to have to work hard on your own. All of my disappointment and surprise could have been avoided if I had known what to expect. In the last chapter, I gave you a list of questions to ask your agent at the time of signing. Make sure you have those written down so you can refer to them. If you get this done on the first day, you'll have a much more productive relationship with your agent.

> **If you're working with a manager, the manager should be the one looking for an agent. If you have an agent and now want to hire a manager, ask the agent for references first. It's important that your agent and manager get along.**

Once I realized how my agent worked, things went much better. I made it a point to visit her office once a week, and she started sending me out on more auditions. That doesn't mean that you should visit your agent every week. Some agents won't like that. It means that you need to find out now what your agent expects from you. The only way to do that is to talk and establish the rules.

When should I look for another agent?

Many actors, if they aren't going out on auditions every day, are too impatient with their agents and want to drop them. For newcomers, it's not always the agent's fault. You'll reap what you sow; if you don't do anything to help, then you might not get many calls. Having said that, there just might come a time when you have to part ways with your agent and these guidelines should help you out.

Before you even consider leaving your agent, study your contract carefully to find out what the legal stipulations are. Contract language varies, but you're typically entitled to leave an agent if he hasn't secured any work for you within a given amount of time.

When you're unknown, you have to work hard to find roles on your own even if you have an agent. But if you've been working hard and your talent agent isn't helping, or if you simply can't build any rapport with the agent, then feel free to shop around for a different one. If your agent consistently sends you out on the same type of assignments, and you feel that you've progressed past those types of roles, then it might be time to look for a different or more powerful agent.

To look for a new agent, you have to go back to step five and start contacting agents again. By this time, though, you should have a good network of actors you've met along the way who might be able to recommend you to someone. Open up your networking notebook and start calling some people. That's one of the many reasons why you need to keep the names and numbers of everyone you meet along the way. It's also possible that you've acquired more credits or changed your headshot. Agents who previously said no might say yes this time.

Help yourself by continuing to work hard

Nearly every newly signed actor complains about not going out on enough auditions, yet they rarely change their own work habits. Instead, they always blame the agent. Once you've signed with an agent, you can help yourself by continuing to show your determination and hard work. This could involve going back to steps four and five and looking for auditions on your own. This time, though, a couple of things will change. You'll need to alter your résumé because you can now add your agent's name and phone number. If you have a manager, you can add the manager's name. Also, you're not going to do mailings to agents anymore. Instead, you can focus on casting directors and auditions.

Sometimes the agents will have you print their contact information on your résumé and sometimes they'll give you a sticker that you can slap on the headshot or résumé with that information on it. When you're submitting to low-budget and no-budget productions, having that agent's name on there might give you some extra credibility. Even though it's low budget, the filmmakers still want the best actors. If they see you have an agent, they'll be more impressed and it just might make the difference in whether or not you get called.

When you're mailing to casting directors, you definitely want to include your agent's information for a couple of reasons. First, it'll show that you're progressing in your career. If you did a previous mailing to a casting director, make sure you mention that you are now represented by your agent. That also serves as a

No talent agent hears about every opportunity. If you want to make it to the top of your agent's list, continue networking and looking for auditions. Any information that you can find for your agent about auditions will help you.

powerful networking tool. That casting director just might know your agent or might meet your agent in the future. If you've been hitting that casting director every two months, you just might score some points. In fact, signing with an agent or manager could be a good reason to do another round of mailings to your casting directors. You could include a note that says, "Just wanted to let you know that I just signed with 'Superstar Talent.'"

If you do sign with an agent or manager, you should consult them about your mailing system. They might want you to stop or they might want you to do something different. Once you're working with someone, keep them informed about what you're doing.

You should also continue to read the trade magazines and entertainment-related websites. With a good eye, you can find a lot of leads for your agent or manager. For example, I recently read an article in *Backstage West* that producer David E. Kelley was looking for new actors for his TV shows *The Agency* and *Boston Public.* The article wasn't very big, but it did mention the name of the casting director. If you see something like that, you should immediately tell your agent or manager. It's possible that they hadn't even heard about this because nobody in Hollywood hears everything all the time.

It's possible that you could read an article about a movie star who has just signed to do a film about dancing. You could fax the article to your agent along with a note that you're a strong dancer. Your agent will appreciate tips like these because you'll be helping her other clients as well. Your agent will notice your commitment, and you will now be on her mind in a good way. If you have a good manager, it's possible that the manager might know some of the people associated with these tips and might be able to get you a personal introduction.

Promote yourself and your agent will help you

This section is not about hiring a publicist or placing ads to promote yourself. Those are options you can consider, and entire books are written about that sort of thing. You can research that area with your agent or manager if you choose; however, you don't need to concern yourself with that right now. For now, I want to outline some ways that you can help build recognition and develop your career so that your agent and manager can sell you more effectively. These ideas include getting into theater, getting into a film festival, producing a great demo reel, working the casting director relationships, developing specific projects, and thinking about your career as a whole. These are the areas that a good manager should assist you with and that an agent will appreciate. If you don't have a manager, you can still do these on your own and you should, because you need a way to set yourself apart from all the other actors your agent works with.

If you can get a good role in a good play, then your agent can help you get seen and your manager can help promote it. Casting directors and their assistants watch plays, as you know. When you land a role in a play and you send out invites, your invite might get tossed because nobody knows you. However, if you mention in the invite that you have an agent, or if your manager invites a casting director or producer personally, suddenly you have more power. Of course you're still going to have to deliver onstage, but at least someone of note is now watching you.

If you're really ambitious, you can do a one-person show and really showcase your talent. Whoopi Goldberg, Anna Deavere

Smith, Chazz Palminteri, and many others rose to fame by first writing their own shows and performing them onstage. Chazz Palminteri's play *A Bronx Tale* was later made into a movie directed by Robert De Niro. Anna Deavere Smith wrote a one-woman play called *Twilight Los Angeles* that brought rave reviews, a movie deal, and many other lucrative offers, including TV shows and book deals. Whoopi Goldberg created a host of memorable characters in one of her first stage works, and those characters are still mentioned whenever she does interviews.

Getting yourself into a quality film is another way to promote your career. That's not as easy as it sounds because you never know what's going to be a great film, but look at a guy like Vince Vaughn, who became a superstar after the film *Swingers* hit theaters. John Travolta had fallen off the face of the earth in the late 1980s and was practically considered a joke. He took a great role in *Pulp Fiction* and suddenly became a "talented" actor again and surpassed all his previous superstardom. Tim Allen was just a working comedian when his HBO special *Men Are Pigs* aired. After that great showcase, he landed the TV show *Home Improvement* and launched a movie career as well.

There are many opportunities to audition for filmmakers who aren't going to pay you. Just because you have an agent now doesn't mean you can't or shouldn't work for free. You should always search for challenging and interesting material because you never know when you might end up in the next *Swingers.*

An agent will love it if you can land great roles onstage or in low-budget films, but he isn't going to go out of his way to find those sorts of projects for you. That falls under the category of "career development" and that's something that a good manager can assist you with. If you have the talent for a one-person theater production, a manager can help you find a writer or director to assist you. Managers work with lots of different talent. It's possible that a manager could manage a writer who's written a great role for a child and your child is managed by the same person. The manager could help develop this script and send it to producers and directors with the intention of casting your child. Agents don't have the time to do this sort of thing.

If you can't get into a quality film, then you might consider making your own. Even though Quentin Tarantino is known in Hollywood as a video store clerk who made it big, he was also a struggling actor just like you. Nine years before *Pulp Fiction* premiered, Quentin was trying to get into the business, and he appeared on three episodes of *The Golden Girls* TV show. He decided to take matters into his own hands and promote himself by making his own movies. I think you could say that he made it.

You should also be updating and adding to your demo reel. In step three of Your Acting Plan I talked about putting together a demo reel as part of the basics. Now might be a good time to do that. You should be keeping video of everything you appear in. Now's the time to spend some money and get that demo reel made. If you've been collecting video footage, revisit step three and learn how to put together your demo reel.

Once you have a demo reel, you can include that information in your letters to casting directors. You don't want to send it unsolicited, but if you mention that you have one, they might be willing to look at it. You should also tell your agent that you have a demo reel. This will give her something else that she can send to casting directors, and it will be one more indicator of just how dedicated and professional you are.

If you're in the union, this would be a good time to consider joining the Academy Players Directory. This is a reference book and website that you can join for a fee. This is one of the few legitimate services that could increase your exposure to agents and casting directors, and it's explained in chapter 4. Although it's not the primary source for casting, many industry professionals actually use this directory as a way to find legitimate actors.

Because this isn't going to bring instant or guaranteed results, it's not something that I recommend you put at the top of your

> Managers for actors typically take 15 percent from actors and 20 percent from musicians, but they are not governed by any recognized authority and are free to do as they wish. This doesn't mean that they are above the law, but they aren't bound by any written code of conduct.

list. At this point, however, when you've got an agent, and you're in the union, and you're looking for every extra edge you can get, it's something that you could consider. For more information, visit www.acadpd.org.

Think "career path"

When actors are starting out, they often get consumed with just finding anything. They want their first agent or their first audition and they're delighted whenever anything happens. That's fine for beginners, but once you get an agent or manager you need to think about a career path.

A career path simply means that you're focusing your energy on a complete presentation. One of my good friends was trying to be a fitness trainer, a screenwriter, a singer, a voice-over artist, and a movie actor. He had some success and made a little money, but he didn't have any clear direction, and he wasn't sure what to do on any given day. We talked about all his abilities and realized that his greatest gift was his voice. It was sort of an awakening for him. After that, he stopped writing, he stopped studying to be a fitness trainer, and he didn't spend as much time looking for auditions. Instead he focused everything on his voice.

He enrolled with one of the top voice-over coaches in New York. He began doing a lot of free voice work as well. Even though he already had a good agent, he hired a manager who helped him produce a new voice-over demo reel and get it into the hands of some bigger agents. Within a year, he was making a

> Hiring a manager is a very personal decision. When inter-
> viewing managers, use the same common sense you'd apply
> to any kind of major personal decision. Ask to talk to other
> clients. Find out what his plans are for your career. Don't just
> sit there and expect your manager to work miracles.

very comfortable living as a voice actor and found time again to go back to his writing. The point is that he stopped thinking about all the things he might do or could do and instead changed his focus on a career as a voice actor.

That might be a lot for you to think about right now, but it could be something to consider at some point in your career. If you're serious about this business, then you need to focus your energy on the things that are most important to you and the things that you can do best. If you don't look twenty years old anymore, then stop wasting your time trying to look twenty and focus on the thirty-year-old roles. If you've been writing a script for five years, either finish it or throw it out. Don't let your life or career become a mishmash of loose ends. A good manager will help guide you in a focused manner.

The advantages of management

If you're the type of person who has a hard time getting orga-
nized and motivated, then a stern and supportive manager might be just what you need to help you do all the things necessary to make it. A manager can also be a wonderful go-between to inter act with your agent or with casting directors. Casting directors don't want to tell actors why they didn't get cast in something, and they don't want actors calling them. A manager is different, though, and he can talk to casting directors about what you did right or wrong in an audition. Also, if you don't want to talk to your agent, a manager can do that for you as well.

The best thing a good manager can do is expand your network. Managers manage, and to do that they have to deal with casting directors, agents, producers, actors, PR personnel, and everyone else connected to the entertainment industry. If they're good, then they'll have plenty of contacts. You won't necessarily have to spend your days and nights buying books and doing research because they can help you target the agents and casting directors they either know personally or do business with. This can give you a lot of time to focus on your acting.

One of the most helpful things a good manager can do is "pitch" you to agents and casting directors. A pitch is nothing more than a conversation in which the manager tries to convince somebody to work with you. If a manager has a relationship with a casting director who's casting a particular role, your manager can meet with that casting director and pitch you by telling her how talented and dedicated you are. No manager will say those things, however, if they aren't true, so you better make sure you can deliver. If a manager has a good reputation, then she'll get people to listen to you. If you can work with a manager who has these abilities, then she might just help you get on the fast track.

Should I get a manager?

The competition in show business is so intense today that's it's nearly impossible to survive without a good manager. All of the big stars have them because even they need people who can help keep their careers alive. You don't need one to begin with, and as I've already mentioned, I wouldn't recommend even looking for one until you have some experience and you know what you're doing. I do think a good manager can be a huge help, so if you want to give it a shot, here's what I would suggest. Don't place acquiring a manager at the top of your list of things to do. I didn't mention managers until step six of the plan, because there is a lot that you can do and learn on your own before you even consider hiring a manager. Plenty of actors have made it without hiring managers. Plenty of actors have also been ripped off and discouraged by unscrupulous managers.

Spend a year on your own first. Follow the steps of Your Acting Plan and try to build experience as you look for an agent. During this time, you'll acquire the knowledge that will help you land a good manager later if you need one. You need to get some exposure to the business and to other actors first. You need to educate yourself.

Except for rare cases of extraordinary beauty or talent, it's unlikely that a very good manager is going to want to work with you if you're a true beginner. He has all the same concerns that an agent has. He wants to see some experience and dedication on your part, so that's why you need to give it a go on your own first before you contact a manager. If you go to a manager with little or no experience and the manager welcomes you with open arms, then it's very possible that you've met someone who is going to disappoint you. If he starts asking you for money and telling you that it's for pictures or other fees, then you need to run away. However, if you just signed a contract with him, you're in a tough position.

When you're just starting out, a good manager is going to tell you to get a job, get some photos done, get into an acting class, and start looking through the audition listings every day to find roles for beginners. In other words, he's going to tell you to follow the steps of Your Acting Plan. If you're organized, you can do this on your own.

Don't get fooled by managers who promise you the world, especially if you're a beginner. Use the same common sense that you would use when hiring anybody. Do your research and read the fine print. If you spend a year in Hollywood following the steps of Your Acting Plan and networking with other actors, then you just might learn enough to avoid getting mistreated by a manager.

> I think an actor has to go out and get some roles and some experience first before going to a manager. Otherwise, what am I managing?
>
> —Ed Goldstone,
> Los Angeles talent manager

A manager is not a cure-all or a guarantee of success. Many beginners want to rush out and get managers before they've even been on a stage. They then become dependent on their managers and lose incentive to investigate things on their own and to try very hard—expecting the manager to do all the work for them. They develop the bad habit of wanting the manager to make everything happen. That can be a dangerous trap to fall into because a manager can't always do much more with a true beginner than the beginner can do on his own. Here's a case in point.

A woman e-mailed me from Las Vegas and said that her son had been solicited by managers who wanted to represent him. They told her that her son wouldn't be able to meet any decent agents or get any auditions without an introduction from someone in the business. This might be true in Los Angeles, but in the smaller markets like Las Vegas it simply isn't the case.

I told the woman that they were intimidating her and that there wasn't much they could do with her child that she couldn't do on her own. I told her that she could mail her child's photo to the local agent just as easily as a manager could. I also reminded her that if her son had a good look, it wouldn't matter if his photo arrived in the jaws of a mule. She took my advice and mailed the photo and résumé on her own. The agent called her immediately and said he needed that type of child on that day.

She took the kid to an audition immediately and booked a role in a print commercial. If she had listened to the manager, she would've paid that manager 15 percent to do exactly the same thing she did.

As a general rule, you should always avoid agents, managers, or any type of salespeople who give you deadlines or tell you that you'll fail without them. Those aren't the words of reputable people. There aren't any regulations regarding talent managers. Although organizations like the Talent Managers Association in Hollywood, whose members adhere to a voluntary code, exist, practically anyone can call himself a manager, and therein lies the danger.

I've heard endless horror stories about actors, singers, and musicians who got into terrible relationships with unethical managers. If you're going to hire a manager, do so very carefully and take all necessary steps to determine the character of the person you're dealing with.

How to hire a talent manager

The best way to hire a manager is to educate yourself and work in the business for at least a year or longer. If you're following the steps of Your Acting Plan and you're going to a regular acting class, auditioning for roles on your own, and networking with other actors, then you're going to meet managers or actors who have managers. It will be impossible not to. Ask questions. Ask for introductions. Ask for references. This is the best way to find a manager. If you've acquired an agent, then ask the agent for a recommendation or ask the other actors whom your agent represents about their managers. If you're not good at networking

Don't fall into the trap of thinking that a manager is going to save your career just because you hire one. You still have to be hungry, organized, and talented.

yet, you can start a letter-writing campaign just like you did for agents.

If you live near a Samuel French bookstore, you can find at least half a dozen different publications that will list managers. These will include names, addresses, phone numbers, and a brief description. One of the better-known publications is the *Agents and Managers* book, which is also available at www.hcdonline. com. You can also look at the Talent Managers Association website at www.talentmanagers.org. This site lists talent managers along with their submission policies and contact information.

You'll want to target the managers just like you did with the agents. That means you want one who lives near you and who handles your type. Once you've found a dozen or so that fit these criteria, use the same type of cover letter that you sent to the agents. Here's a sample:

> Dear Manager,
>
> I'm a dedicated actor currently studying at the Acting Naturally workshop in Hollywood. I just booked my third independent film and I now have a growing demo reel. I'm looking for a manager and would like to enlist your services. If you'd like to work with my type, please call now and we'll start taking my career to a new level.
>
> Sincerely,
> *John Bolin*

That's all you need. Enclose a headshot and résumé and mail it in a large envelope. As always, if they're interested, they'll call you.

What you don't want to do is sit at home and search the Web for sites that say, "Get discovered today at Oblio Talent Management." It's also a bad idea to go through the phone book to find a manager without doing anything else about your career. If you have no experience and no training, then only a scam artist is going to talk to you, and you'll soon be parting with your money.

Jamie-Lynn Sigler, star of *The Sopranos,* was acting in plays for years around New York and New Jersey before she acquired a manager. Until that time, she would look for auditions on her own and her mom would escort her to the auditions. One of her cast mates had a manager, and he introduced his manager to Jamie-Lynn, who then signed with the same manager. This is the best way to do it because it's coming from a trusted, reputable source.

ACTION POINTS

- Establish a clear set of rules for working with your agent.
- Understand that managers help mold your talent so that agents can sell your talent.
- It's time to start thinking "career path."
- If you've educated yourself and you're ready for a manager, approach him or her carefully just like you would an agent, and try to find one who will help you get to the next level.

DAILY GOALS

Now your goals involve a lot of thinking. Think about the focus of your career and go back through the steps of the plan and make sure you're doing everything you can. You should also think about your relationship with your agent. Are the rules clear to both of you? Also, are you doing everything you possibly can to help your agent and to prove how dedicated and determined you are? If you have questions or doubts concerning your relationship with your agent, then make an appointment to meet with her, or make a decision to change your behavior and recommit yourself.

Finally, I want you to consider one thing you can do to get your career to the next level. I gave you some suggestions in this chapter, but they are not the only ways to give yourself a boost. This is gut check time. If things aren't happening for you at this point, you might give up and quit. If you have what it takes, however, you'll find the strength to go further. Finding that strength is a wonderful way of answering the question, "What did you do today to advance your acting career?"

10

STEP SEVEN:
ALWAYS NETWORKING

Y OU have really educated yourself greatly up to this point. You've not only prepared yourself to become an actor, you've learned what agents and managers do, and you've also learned some new ways to promote yourself and advance your career. If you've followed all the steps up to this point, then you've accomplished quite a bit and you should know a great deal more than when you started. Now I'm going to introduce you to the most important and effective method of progressing as an actor. Nothing in your acting education is as important as the concept of networking.

"Hang out with nine losers, and you'll be the tenth loser. Hang out with nine winners, and you'll be the tenth winner. Hang out with nine out-of-work actors, and you'll be the tenth out-of-work actor. Hang out with nine working actors, and you'll be the tenth working actor." A working actor said this to me once, and I'll never forget these valuable words.

I debated making this the first chapter of the book because I think it's the most important, but I feared that too many actors

wouldn't take it seriously and they'd skip to the sections on finding agents and auditions. So instead of putting it at the front, I'm
just going to ask you to read it twice. You will never stop networking in this business, and I can't possibly overstate to you
how much it will help your chances as an actor.

When I moved to Los Angeles, everyone told me that I had to
network in order to get ahead. I hated networking. I didn't
believe in it. Whenever someone told me to network, or whenever I read some advice column that talked about networking, I
shrugged it off. I didn't think that talking to people was the way
to get ahead. I thought I could just read a book or pay a manager
or something like that and I would be discovered. I learned the
hard way that networking is everything in this business, and it's
one of the most important steps for advancing your career.

In this chapter, I explain networking and give you some solid
techniques that you can use to start meeting people today. I also
demonstrate how where you live, the job you do, and the social
life you enjoy can all affect your networking efforts.

If you want to win the lottery, buy lots of tickets

Networking in this business is like playing the lottery. If
you want to increase your chances of winning the lottery,
you have to buy lots of tickets. Every person you meet
in this business is like another ticket. Teachers, actors,
agents—they're all tickets that will increase your chances
of getting discovered. You can never network with too
many people in this business. Guys like James Gandolfini
and Tommy Lee Jones just stuck with it and kept buying
lottery tickets for years and years until they won.

—Chris Fenton, former William Morris
talent agent and current talent
manager

I don't know how to explain it any better than Chris just did. Actors who don't network while hoping to get discovered are like people who don't buy lottery tickets and hope to win the lottery. If getting discovered is the lottery that you're hoping to win, ask yourself how many lottery tickets you've purchased. Buying this book is ticket number one, but you need to buy a thousand more tickets if you want a good chance at winning. What other tickets have you purchased? Have you moved to Los Angeles or New York? Are you in a class? Have you auditioned for anything yet? Those are all tickets waiting to be purchased by you.

If this is a little too abstract for you to completely understand, let's revisit the casting process briefly to see how this applies. Someone is going to get cast in something tomorrow. Roles are cast every day, so it's safe to say that someone somewhere is going to get cast in something. A producer will make a decision and say, "This is the actor I want." The casting director will then call an agent and say, "They want your client for the role." The agent will then call the actor and say, "Guess what. You got it." The actor will then call his acting teacher and say, "I just got the part!" Look at all those people involved, and those are just the main players. Let's dig deeper and look at all the lottery tickets involved in the casting of that one role.

The actor had to move to Los Angeles (1 ticket). To do that, she called a friend and asked for a place to crash (2 tickets). Once she found a job she started asking her coworkers about acting workshops (3 tickets). They gave her some recommendations. She went to a workshop and met a good acting teacher (4 tickets). In the class, she talked with other actors who told her about various auditions (5, 6, 7 tickets). She looked through all the audition sources listed in step four and started finding small acting jobs (8, 9, 10 tickets). At her first acting job she talked with another actor about an agent (11 tickets). That actor introduced her to his agent and she got signed (12 tickets). That agent started sending her out on jobs and she auditioned for a casting director who didn't hire her, even though she thought she was a good actor (13 tickets). That casting director went out to dinner that night and talked to another casting director who was casting a new TV show. She said to her friend, "I just auditioned this girl who would be perfect for that role you're casting" (14 tickets). The casting director called the agent. The agent called the actor and the actor auditioned for the new casting director.

This is exactly how actors get cast. There were fourteen tickets involved, and that was an extremely simple example. It might take an actor years to get cast in something substantial, and there could easily be a thousand lottery tickets purchased along the way. Any actor who ever got cast in anything will be able to trace all the steps and all the people who helped her get to that point where someone said, "You got the role." It will all be the result of networking and staying active, persistent, and determined.

Let's look at an example of someone who didn't win the acting lottery. Here's what he did. He got a great job in Denver as a personnel director and bought a nice car. He couldn't just quit his job because he had to make payments on the car. He really wanted to be an actor but he worried too much about giving up everything and moving to Los Angeles. Instead of moving or joining an acting class, he just wished really hard that he was famous. Nobody ever called him to tell him that he just got the part. So instead, he joined some website that promised he would be discovered by thousands of casting directors if he signed up and paid the fee. So he bought the online portfolio and uploaded his picture. Months

> **Good actors are usually good at networking. A good networker has to be determined, smart, creative, and unafraid to talk to people. Those are the same qualities of a fine actor.**

went by and nothing happened. In other words, he bought one lottery ticket, but it turned out to be counterfeit.

I want you to start thinking about buying one lottery ticket each day or each week. A lottery ticket is someone related to show business who can reveal a piece of information that will bring you closer to getting an agent or getting an audition.

It's all about relationships

Ask any decent talent agent where she gets the majority of her actors and she'll say, "From personal referrals." Put yourself in the talent agent's position for a moment. Every day you receive a hundred headshots and résumés from new actors. They all say the same thing. "Hi, I'm a new actor looking for representation. Please call if interested." Every day it's the same. Each actor has performed in a few plays and student films and has a decent headshot. They're all essentially the same. You look at one particular headshot and the girl looks like a Reese Witherspoon type. You don't have any actors of that type, but you still don't call her because you already have enough to do.

Later that day, one of your actors comes in to drop off a stack of headshots and he says, "I met this girl in my acting class last night who's looking for an agent. Do you think you could meet her?" You say, "What's she like?" The actor says, "We did a scene together in class and she really blew me away. This girl can act. She's like a Reese Witherspoon type." The actor hands you her headshot and you see that it's the same girl who mailed you her résumé, but now you want to meet her. Why?

You want to meet her because she has now come with a personal recommendation. You trust your actor's judgment, and you know that he doesn't come into the office every day trying to sign up his friends who are actors. That is the value of networking. A personal introduction will get you in the door much more effectively than an unsolicited mailing. This doesn't mean

MY TOP FIVE NETWORKING SITUATIONS

1. **Movie sets**
2. **Acting classes**
3. **Film festivals**
4. **Filmmaking schools**
5. **Professional networking groups**

that you should stop doing your mailings. If you don't have an agent, you still need to mail out headshots. What I want you to realize is that you need to meet people. While you're doing your mailings you need to network.

The reason I was so reluctant to network when I moved to Los Angeles was that I never realized how effective and important it was. I was shy, too, which didn't make it any easier, but I have discovered that you're only limited by your courage and creativity. I have devised a system of networking that will help you reach your goals no matter where you live or who you know. If you have the determination, you can meet the people you want using the power of three.

The power of three

People are like websites in that we're all connected. You just have to find the links. If you started at www.myactingagent. com and wanted to get to some other website, all you'd have to do is keep clicking links until you got to your new destination. Meeting people can be done in the same manner. Just like the Web, it doesn't matter where you start.

This is a sure way to meet people and build your network of contacts. Imagine you want to meet a talent agent. Pick the person you know who is the closest to the film industry. If you're in Hollywood, it could be your friend, neighbor, coworker, or family member. If you live in Austin, Texas, it could be the soundman at your favorite bar. It doesn't matter where you start. Talk to that person about your plans and desires and ask him to give you the names of three people you could talk to who might be able to help you out.

His first reaction might be, "I don't know anybody." Prod him. Tell him it doesn't have to be someone famous. It just has to be someone who knows more than he does. Then he might say, "Well, I got a friend whose sister moved to New York last year." That's great. Get the name and number and contact the next person. When you contact the next person, drop the name of the person who referred you. This way you'll be maintaining a line of personal references.

When you talk to the next person, do the same thing again. Tell her what you're looking for and ask for the names of three people you could talk to. If you keep doing this and never give up, you're going to reach your networking goal eventually. You have to put the word out there and put the energy out there. If you're too shy, then take the acting tests again until you find your courage. It's all in your hands. If you hit a dead end, just start talking to someone else.

If you live in Los Angeles or New York, it's really easy to network because so many people are connected to the business. Here's a perfect example of what I'm talking about.

I was in a restaurant with an actor who had come to me to discuss managing her career. She had just arrived in town from New Jersey and didn't know much about the business. I began explaining how to network, and a guy sitting at the next table

If you're a student, regardless of your level of study, approach a guidance counselor and ask him if there is someone he could introduce you to who knows something about the entertainment business. Guidance counselors are excellent starting points because it's their job to help you network.

interrupted us and said, "He's giving you some pretty good advice." We began talking with the guy, and it turned out he was from New Jersey as well. He was an actor who had just finished shooting a film at the USC film school.

Because the young woman didn't have a headshot or business card yet, I asked the guy if he would take her e-mail address and e-mail her when his film had its premiere. This wasn't going to be a major studio premiere, but all films get shown somewhere at some time. The actor agreed and took the e-mail address. Here's what I told her to do next.

By the time that film gets edited and is ready to be shown, she'll have a headshot and résumé together. When she goes to that premiere, she'll be in a room full of actors and filmmakers. All premieres come with some type of party before or after. At that party she can meet the filmmaker and hand him her headshot and say, "I loved your movie; consider me for your next project."

She doesn't put him on the spot. She gives him a nice compliment, and she makes her first connection. See how easy that was? "But Pete, I'm not gonna get anywhere talking to student filmmakers." Yes, you will! When you're starting out, you need to get credits. Student filmmakers need actors who'll work for free. Most major directors working today were student filmmakers at some point.

Another point to keep in mind is that those student filmmakers are going to try to sell themselves. They're going to send their films to festivals, agents, and studios. If you're in that film, then you're going to be seen by all those people, too, and you just might catch someone's eye.

Your Networking Tools

You need to have a contact book and to start filling it with entries. Go back to your notebook and create a new tab called "Networking." Whenever you meet someone with whom you network, enter their name along with what they do and their contact info.

Here are some sample entries; I didn't list phone numbers or e-mails, but it's important for you to get their contact information.

Steve Signore: Met at coffee shop. Actor.
Karen Marion: Makeup artist. Met at Chuck E. Cheese.
Keith Nelson: Met at copy shop. Camera operator. Call next month about film.
April Robbins: Met on train. In a play next month at Fritz Theater.

It would also be good to have some business cards. Actors in Hollywood get business cards made with their headshots on them. They can easily hand them out while networking. I went to a film screening at a coffee shop in Hollywood and began talking to a woman about my book and website. She promptly reached into her bag and pulled out a postcard that had her headshot on it. On the other side was information regarding a play in which she was performing. That's a well-prepared actress.

One day I went to a voice-over recording class to learn about the voice recording business. There were ten actors in the class, and they spent a few hours practicing voice recordings. When it was over, three of the actors took out their business cards and handed them to everyone in the room. It was easy to see who the three most determined and organized actors were. By handing out those cards, they were each collecting lottery tickets. It turns out that a month later, someone told me that they were

Business cards, with or without your picture, are available on the Web and at local print shops for ridiculously low prices. It will help your networking efforts tremendously to have some with you at all times.

casting an announcer for a radio spot. I retrieved one of those cards I collected and handed it to her. I told her that I'd heard that guy perform and he was very good.

How to Network

Networking is nothing more than having a conversation. Ask questions. Be polite and pleasant. Don't run around shoving your photo in people's faces and saying, "Make me a star." To network efficiently, you have to know when to sell yourself and when to hold off. To do this, you have to realize when you've put yourself in a position to get noticed. Don't take advantage of friends. Here's an example.

You discover that one of the actors in your acting class works as an agent's assistant. Should you network with him? Absolutely, but keep these points in mind. If your friend is the same type as you, then don't ask him to submit you to his agent. Agents don't want two beginning actors who are the same type. Don't push any contact to do something they're not comfortable with. If your friend doesn't want to introduce you, then accept that and move on. Don't put him on the spot. You want to be diligent, but you can't afford to appear pushy. Pushy actors are a big turnoff to everyone.

If you meet someone who works for an agent, don't start in with asking for a meeting, especially if they've never seen you act. That's going too far. However, you could ask about his relationship with the agency. Ask him what its submission policy is and how many actors it represents. Ask if it would be appropriate to have him walk your photo into the agent. That way his relationship with the agent isn't strained. He can hand the photo to the agent and say, "This is my friend." If the agent says no, don't ask your friend to get an explanation, and don't ask your friend if he can try again. That friend can still help you out by

An agent's assistant in Hollywood began taking down the e-mail addresses of all the people he dealt with in the industry. This included agents, assistants, talent, and more. Over time, his list grew so big and important that he later had several agencies bidding for his service just to have access to his contacts.

sharing information about certain auditions and other important things that go on at an agency.

If you meet an agent at a party, restaurant, or some other place, don't ask her to be your agent and don't ask her for a meeting. That's putting her on the spot before she's even had a chance to think. Instead, ask her what the proper procedure is for submitting to her for representation. Whatever she tells you is what you'll do. If she asks you to call or send in a letter, make sure to reference this meeting when you do so. Be respectful, professional, and courteous, and you'll be treated fairly. If you come off as too pushy, then she'll run away from you.

Networking events

A networking event is anything that puts you in contact with people related to the entertainment industry. For serious actors, every waking moment is a networking event, but some things are particularly made for networking. These events could include seminars by agents or managers, film festivals, plays, writers' groups and acting workshops, and even class reunions. In New York and Los Angeles, they happen every day. In other places they aren't as frequent, but they do occur. It's up to you to find them. By reading the trade magazines, entertainment websites, school notices, and message boards, you can find these. Make it a habit to read the arts section of your local newspapers. If you live in an area that sells *Backstage,* start subscribing to it.

> Join your college alumni group. Most colleges have alumni
> organizations in the major cities. Find yours and start
> networking. College alumni love to help each other out.
> I'm a proud member of the Texas Exes, and I'm always
> talking with my fellow alumni in the business.

On your calendar, you need to schedule at least one networking event each month. This should be something that puts you
in touch with somebody in the acting world. If you live in a
small town, you can go see a play somewhere. I'm always
attending film premieres and seminars from agents and producers. One of my favorite sources for seminars is The Learning
Annex; check out their site at www.learningannex.com.

As I'm writing this, I clicked on The Learning Annex website
to see what was going on in my area. Here's an actual listing for
a class they're holding.

Green Light Your Project
with
PANEL OF INDUSTRY EXPERTS
* This is the Pitching Event That Could Launch Your Career! *

The best pitch gets the movie made. With the right approach,
you could get the green light and be on your way to a successful career as a writer, filmmaker, or producer.

Lights! Cameras! Financing!

Come learn from our experts how to pitch your project,
get a development deal, and make the movie.

Panelists include:

- Shaun Redick, literary agent, I.C.M.
- Alex Pereira, agents assistant, I.C.M.
- Zach Tann, of Zide Perry
- Ivan Oyco, supervisor of acquisitions,
  Disney/Buena Vista

- Plus: A special surprise guest!
- *Moderator:* Page Ostrow, president of Ostrow & Company. She's arranged the global financing and sold the international license rights to over 70 feature films.

Bonus: Attendees will have the chance to do a short (25 words or less) pitch to our panel. Be sure to bring your ideas and submissions and get ready for plenty of feedback! The best pitch wins a free consultation with Ostrow & Company. Note: Panelists are not to be solicited.

Now that's what I call a networking event. You'll be standing in the same room with agents from ICM. For those of you who don't know talent agencies, ICM is considered one of the big five. They represent some of the top talent in Hollywood. It's true that this isn't exactly for actors, but it's all related. Everyone in attendance is going to be an aspiring filmmaker, actor, or writer. When you arrive and find your seat, start talking with the other attendees and exchange cards.

Many colleges invite speakers from the entertainment industry. When I was at the University of Texas, I went to listen to a speech from Jack Valenti, chairman of the Motion Picture Association of America. Jack gave an entertaining and inspirational speech that encouraged me to move to Hollywood. I didn't speak with him personally and I didn't exchange cards with anyone, but I exposed myself to the industry and found lots of inspiration and encouragement. That's always the very least that can happen.

Each year in Hollywood and New York, *Backstage* sponsors an event called *Actorfest.* It's a weekend-long event in which vendors from the acting industry set up booths to advertise their products to actors. It's a gathering of acting teachers, headshot photographers, voice-over coaches, website companies, and just about everything else related to acting. Seminars are also held throughout the day by casting directors, talent agents, and other industry professionals who will give talks about how to get into the business. It usually happens around May in Los Angeles and October in New York. Details can be found at www.backstage.com.

Specific networking examples that you can do today

As I mentioned previously, you're only limited by your courage and creativity. When you live in a major city, networking opportunities are everywhere. Smaller cities don't have as many, but they still have enough to help you. I'm going to list some very specific examples that you can use no matter where you live. These are just some of the many ways to network.

Your local theater

This networking opportunity will work no matter where you live. Find a small theater in your town. If there isn't a theater in your town, go to the next town that has one. The theater will have some kind of bulletin board near the entry or in the lobby. There will probably be an office as well. Walk into the theater and look around. Find that bulletin board. On that bulletin board you'll see ads for acting classes, auditions, and other acting-related items.

Find something in there that will connect you with somebody. If there's a class listed, sign up for it. If an audition is coming up, sign up for it even if you think you aren't ready or aren't right for the part. Do it anyway. Talk to the manager about upcoming events. Ask the manager when rehearsals are for the current production and ask if you could watch a rehearsal. You might not be allowed to watch, but if you can at least find out the rehearsal time, then you'll know when the actors are going to show up.

Once rehearsal is over, introduce yourself to the actors and ask about agents, filmmaking opportunities, and classes. You're bound to find at least one actor in the bunch who'll answer your questions. They know what's going on in the town, and they are your best source of information for your area.

Film Festivals

Just about every major city in the world has a film festival now. As I search the Web today, I notice there are eight film festivals in the United States in the month of August alone. The most obscure are in Cincinnati, Ohio, and Crested Butte, Colorado. If you live anywhere near those cities, here's what you can do.

Every film festival has a website. Go to the website and research all the films and filmmakers. Find something that catches your attention. Maybe there's a filmmaker from nearby. Maybe there's a particular subject that you like. Make a list of the films you want to see and the people you want to meet. Pack up your headshots and go to the festival. Maybe it's in your town and you just drive fifteen minutes to the theater. Maybe it's eight hours away and you have to get a motel for the night or nights. Whatever it takes, do it. Even if you don't have headshots, go anyway.

All film festivals have opening night ceremonies and parties and sometimes a seminar or two. After each screening there are usually press conferences along with a Q & A session with the filmmakers. Find out where these are and go to them. They will be filled with filmmakers, agents, producers, and actors. Talk to people about the films you've seen at the festival or the films you're going to see. Before you know it, you'll be exchanging business cards and making contacts. I can't tell you exactly what will happen, but something will happen if you put yourself into that situation.

"But Pete, what do I actually say to these people?" There aren't any rules about what you can and can't say. My advice is don't be too pushy. You don't want to be known as that girl who goes around begging everyone to be in their movie. Talk about anything, but as long as you're at the film festival, you might as well talk about films. Ask them why they're there and what they're doing. They'll probably ask you the same. If you meet someone related to a project, just ask if you could "get involved" in the next project. That's all you have to say. That way you're being generous, curious, and not too pushy. Getting involved could mean anything from acting to carrying equipment. In either case, you'll be making friends and getting closer to the industry, and that's a great place to start.

At the very least, you'll probably find some inspiration. If you're passionate about film and acting like I am, then you'll come home from your trip and you'll be filled with ideas and hope. You'll be so excited. You'll say, "Wow, I just met some cool filmmakers and found out that they're regular people just like me. I gotta make a movie. I gotta get involved."

ACTUAL NETWORKING GROUPS

A networking group doesn't necessarily have to be focused on acting. I found a real estate investment group online and I went to a meeting. As everyone introduced themselves, I discovered that two in the group were actors and one was a director. Naturally I got their cards and gave them mine. I entered their info in my book, too. I have remained friends with those people to this day.

Other groups meet strictly for networking purposes. I can't even list all the networking groups in Los Angeles. My wife joined a networking group for her web design business. It's a

A quick search on the Net will locate a film festival near you. These are great networking events because they're filled with actors, directors, agents, and producers.

group of fourteen people and each represents a different segment of business. One is a lawyer, one is a web designer, one is a massage therapist. The idea is that they all try to assist one another in their business endeavors. If you joined a networking group like that, you might find that the lawyer knows some agents and that the massage therapist knows some directors.

The best way to find these groups is by visiting message boards and bookstores, and by looking through your local paper in the arts or community sections. Most schools list this information on bulletin boards and in newsletters. No matter what your interest or where you live, you can find some kind of group on the Internet that is willing to talk about it.

With the advent of digital filmmaking, film groups are popping up all over the country. If you live in the big cities, you can throw a rock and find one of these. These are groups of passionate artists who spend their free time making movies. They always need actors and assistants. I list various film groups on my website, but you can also find them by checking the arts section of your local paper. Nearly every college has film groups of some sort. Look for group meetings and screenings of small films. That's where these people gather.

Many of these groups have websites. In Los Angeles there is the Filmmakers Alliance. There's another group called Group101 Films that has chapters across the country. Visit their websites and get on their mailing lists. They'll send you information on auditions and screenings.

INTERNSHIPS

Internships are one of the best ways to see what goes on inside of show business. Casting directors, talent agents, theater companies, and production companies are often looking for interns to come and work for free in exchange for learning the business. This is a fantastic idea and one that few beginners take advantage of.

To find these opportunities, check with your local schools. Typically colleges offer some kind of internships. If you're currently enrolled in school, check to see what's available.

ALUMNI ASSOCIATIONS

If you've graduated from college, join your alumni association and visit the New York or Los Angeles chapters. You'll be surprised how many people from across the world end up working in the entertainment business. Members of alumni associations exist only to network and socialize, so if someone in your alumni association happens to be working in show business, that's a guaranteed introduction to the people you need to meet. Take advantage of it.

BECOME A PA

The fastest way to meet people in the business is to get involved in a movie production. The best part about this opportunity is that it's so easy to do. I guarantee that you could move to Los Angeles or New York and begin working on a movie in one week. Just follow this advice. Become a PA.

A PA is a "Production Assistant." PAs are needed every day, and it's the easiest job to get. It probably won't pay any money, but what it will pay you in connections and knowledge is well worth it. Here's how you do it.

If you're in Los Angeles or New York, just get a copy of *Backstage*. You can also look on its website, www.backstage.com. Look through the casting notices and help wanted section. You will soon find at least a dozen filmmakers looking for PAs. You call or e-mail them and say, "I want to be a PA." You'll probably get hired right over the phone. Another great site for finding PA work is www.mandy.com.

If you live in a smaller town, then you have to find a film production company or a film group. You can do this by going to your state's film commission website and looking up the links to the local production companies. Call the companies and tell them you want to be a PA on their next production. You can also do this by going to a local university's film department. Even if you're not a student, they'll usually accept volunteers. Every film production needs PAs. There are never enough of them.

What you'll do as a PA is run errands, carry things, fix things, serve food, and just about anything else that the filmmaker needs you to do. If something happens to the sound guy, you might end up holding a microphone. You might even end up as an extra. You'll work long hours for little or no pay, but you'll gain as much knowledge in one weekend on a film set than you would in a full semester at most colleges.

The best benefit is that you'll see exactly how a film gets made. If you're working on a no-budget film with five crew members, you're going to see the exact same process that you would see on a $100 million budget film with major stars and eighty crew members. The only difference is the number of people and all the extra goodies that a big budget buys. The actual shooting process is exactly the same.

When the director yells, "Action," the set will be quiet and you'll get to see how the actors react. You'll have a moment of silence to imagine what you would do if you were the actor. You'll get to see the distractions, the problems, the improvising, the direction, and everything else that happens when you're on a set.

This is also a fantastic networking opportunity. You'll be able to talk to the actors about what classes they take, who their agents are, and how to get auditions. You'll be able to tell everyone that you're an actor. Other people on the crew will be making movies at some point, too, and they might want to use you. The director will keep you in mind as well, and you just might get a role if someone drops out or if you seem especially interesting.

Maybe your interest is in lighting or camera work. If that's the case, you can talk to the camera operator and his assistants. In short, all your questions about the business and local opportunities can be answered right there. You'll have a group of experts who are willing to talk to you. That's what you get in exchange for helping out. Most important, though, you'll get the excitement and inspiration that comes with being on a movie set.

If you get on a set as a PA or even as an actor, make sure you bring your notebook. You're going to want to collect everyone's cards and contact information. You're also going to want to hand out your card to everyone. Maybe you'll be on another set one day and the director will say, "Our makeup person dropped out." You can save the day by going through your book and finding the contact info for the makeup people you've worked with. Soon, you'll become more and more valuable.

AGENTS' ASSISTANTS

Believe it or not, the most powerful people in Hollywood are talent agents' assistants. These are usually aspiring agents and actors right out of college working their first entertainment jobs. They know everything. They all talk with one another, and they all know which director needs a script, and who's looking for what actors. They know where all the auditions are, too. The best thing about them is that, unlike agents, these people will actually talk to you. So how do you meet these people? It's not that hard. You simply need to get out of the house.

Get on the entertainment mailing lists. Find out where the talent agencies are and go to the restaurants nearby. Talk to the

Don't limit your networking efforts to strictly acting-related activities. You can find great contacts in investment clubs, real estate clubs, computer clubs, and more. It's easy, because people outside of show business love talking about the people they know who are in it or close to it.

waiters and bartenders. I could almost guarantee that they know the name of an assistant. When you talk to them, use the power of three and you'll soon be making connections. Talk to everyone on the movie sets that you go to. Whenever you go to an audition, get the name of the assistant who's checking in the talent. The chances are good that she'll be a casting director someday.

Why are the assistants more powerful than the agents? First, the assistants open the mail and send the mail while the agents are making deals. The assistants know exactly what's going on. Second, the assistants are also usually younger and more approachable. When the agents go out, they're usually with friends or family and aren't interested in talking to every waiter who wants to be an actor. They're trying to avoid actors in some cases. Assistants, on the other hand, are usually doing the same things that actors are doing. That is, they're going out to coffeehouses, bookstores, yoga studios, health clubs, theaters, and nightclubs. They're on the lookout for new talent, too.

Remember that these assistants want to be agents some day, and many of them will. That's where agents come from. They'd love to discover some new talent and maybe even sign their first client.

During one of my acting workshops, a college student, who was in Los Angeles for the summer, announced that he was interning at an agency. All the smart people in the class gave him their headshot and résumé and asked him to submit them to the agency. He gladly obliged.

PRODUCERS

One of the best-kept secrets in Hollywood is networking with TV and film producers. Only the most advanced actors ever think of it, and this is why it's so powerful. Most actors are trying to meet agents and casting directors. Busy agents and casting directors often have their defenses up. If you tell them you're an

KILLER NETWORKING TIP!

Many film festivals need volunteers. You get to attend the festival and network for free. It's true that you'll have to do some work, but it's not very strenuous and you'll get access to everything.

actor, they almost automatically shut you down because they see so many actors. They can be difficult to approach because every actor who does so has the same intention: "Hire me!" That's a natural intention and there's nothing wrong with it. I'm just saying that agents and casting directors can get pretty jaded by the whole process, and they don't have the time or desire to talk to another beginner.

On the other hand, actors rarely badger producers, and thus they can be much more receptive. Producers are usually approached by writers, agents, and other producers, but relatively speaking very few actors try to contact producers. This is ironic because it's the producer who usually has the final say in everything—including casting!

If a casting director has just auditioned a hundred actors and then she sees your picture in a pile on her desk, she's not likely to call you because she already has enough actors to choose from and she doesn't know you. If you call her anonymously, she'll probably just shut you down before you even finish a sentence.

As I said, producers are not as jaded. Imagine you meet a producer and make a great impression. Then the producer, who rarely gets approached by actors, calls the casting director and says, "I want you to give this actor an audition." The casting director has to oblige because she's working for the producer.

You can meet producers by using the same techniques I've already mentioned in this chapter. Don't focus all your energy on agents and casting directors. Trade magazines like the ones I

> **You can get contact information for producers in the Holly-
> wood Creative Directive Directory available at www.books
> aboutacting.com. These are nationwide listings of all the
> players in the entertainment industry. Start learning their
> names. Also, check the credits of your favorite films and
> TV shows to find out who the producers are.**

mentioned earlier in the chapter mention producers' names all
the time. They're everywhere. Producer so-and-so just signed a
three-picture deal with this studio. Producer Betty is casting a
role for her sitcom. Producer Hal has just secured financing for
a movie about a swimmer. These are the kinds of tips you can
use in your letters and phone calls to contact these people and
introduce yourself.

ACTING WORKSHOPS

Acting workshops are full of actors. The instructors usually have
some knowledge about the business as well. These are the kinds
of people you want to associate with. Don't think of your fellow
actors as competitors. Instead, think of them as your lottery tickets. A female actor might come to class and announce that she
heard about an audition for male actors. Try to find a class that
encourages networking. In all of my workshops, I tried to set
aside at least twenty to thirty minutes in each class to discuss the
business of acting, during which the actors could share networking adventures and ideas.

It's also important to be well trained. I worked briefly with an
actor who was a master at networking. He made amazing contacts and was always taking meetings, handing out his photos,
and going to auditions. His problem was that he took one eight-
week acting course and he simply wasn't a very good actor. Even
though he had all these great contacts, they didn't do him any
good because he couldn't deliver when they said, "Action!"

In every acting workshop there's always that one actor who seems to know everything that's going on. She hears about all the auditions, seminars, gossip, and more. Get to know that person in your workshop.

BOOKSTORES

I go to a bookstore almost every week, and it's amazingly simple to meet people in these places. The Samuel French bookstore is especially helpful because it's dedicated to acting. Nearly any acting-related book, including most plays, scripts, and directories, can be found there. If you live near a Samuel French bookstore, just walk in and you'll be in the presence of at least a dozen actors immediately. Don't be shy about asking questions. The employees especially will be able to tell you what the best books are for your needs. They can also recommend local classes, photographers, and groups.

If you don't have a Samuel French in your area, just go to the acting section of any major bookstore and you'll bump into someone who shares your interests. Introduce yourself. Ask them where they are with their career. Ask them which websites they visit, which books they recommend, and what networking they've done. You just might make a great connection. While you're there, look through a book or two. You might pick up a tip about auditioning, networking, or acting.

ACTUAL AUDITIONS AND FILM SHOOTS

When you start going out on auditions, you're going to meet actors and casting directors. Make sure you're bringing your book and taking names. Take down the name and address of each casting director you meet. Any casting director you audition for should go into your book and should be placed on your mailing list. You'll want to mail a postcard to that person every two months. Even if she didn't cast you, you still need to contact her again. Once she has seen you, she'll know what you can do, and by sending her a reminder, you just might get called in to audition for something else.

If you ever do extra work, you'll meet dozens of people with whom you should network. Talk to them and get their cards. I've made some of my best connections while doing extra work. I've met other extras who were filmmakers and writers. I've even handed out flyers for plays that I was in while working as an extra.

THE JOB THAT YOU DO

Some jobs are better for networking than others, and many actors choose jobs specifically for access to the entertainment industry. There are jobs that can put you very close to the action, but you must realize how to handle such a situation.

When I worked as a bartender at The Beverly Hills Hotel, there were a few bartenders and waiters who thought they were going to talk with agents each day and make great contacts. Agents and stars certainly came in, but employees were strictly forbidden from approaching them about such opportunities. That doesn't mean that networking couldn't be done and that contacts couldn't be made. It simply means that actors have to know how to handle the situation.

In my years in the restaurant business, I never saw a situation where a waiter or bartender was able to approach an agent or producer and then request representation or a meeting. Restaurant personnel who think they're going to be able to do this are the ones who get fired. Don't make the mistake of thinking you can move to New York or Los Angeles, get a job at a restaurant, and start handing out headshots to the patrons. It doesn't work that way.

Before he became the star of hits like *Saving Private Ryan* and *The Brothers McMullen*, Edward Burns worked as a PA for the TV show *Entertainment Tonight*.

A waiter who regularly waits on agents and casting directors is going to make more connections if he's a star waiter. That is, if he's polite, charming, courteous, and entertaining, then the people he's waiting on will grow to like him and be interested in him. They might even ask if he's an actor. Later, if he sends a letter to that agent or shows up in that casting director's office, the agent or casting director will have some knowledge and respect for him and might be willing to see him.

If you're going to take a restaurant job for networking opportunities, keep in mind that it's your coworkers you'll be networking with and not necessarily the patrons. It's a running joke that the waiters and bartenders in Los Angeles are all actors, and most of them are. It's a flexible job that pays well and allows actors to audition during the day. Once you start talking to coworkers you'll find out about agents, auditions, classes, and any other acting-related information you might be seeking.

One of the first jobs I took when I moved to Los Angeles was that of a tour guide at Universal Studios. I didn't gain access to Steven Spielberg, but I was hanging out with dozens of actors every day who constantly discussed projects, ideas, opportunities, and events. It was a great situation in which to learn, and by being on the Universal Studios lot each day, I was always inspired and excited.

Many actors take jobs as security officers at studios for networking opportunities. Being on the lot of any studio provides lots of valuable information, and most studios grant employees who they know are actors certain privileges. For instance, an actor working at a studio can usually drop off headshots at the various production companies and casting agencies that have offices in those studios. That's a huge advantage. But just like the restaurant business, a studio is not going to allow its employees to approach TV or movie stars and say, "Hi, I'm an actor, can you help me?" So you have to be smart about your networking.

DON'T FORGET THE BASICS

I want to remind you how important it is to have completed the basics of step three before you try approaching agents or their assistants. Imagine you go to a coffee shop or bookstore one night and you start talking with someone and you realize she's an agent's assistant. What are you going to say? If you don't have a résumé, some training, and at least a few credits under your belt, you have nothing to offer. Nothing will ruin your credibility as fast as saying, "Uh, um, yeah, I'm gonna get some headshots some day, I just haven't gotten around to it yet." Just meeting somebody isn't enough. You have to be able to deliver the goods.

If you meet someone by chance and you simply haven't done anything yet, don't try to lie your way through it. It's better to say "I just got into town and haven't done a thing yet" than it is to say "I'll get some photos done someday." There are too many actors who plan on getting photos done "someday," and they aren't taken seriously.

It's all about you

Regardless of the job you do or where you go to network, the most important element is your ability to hold a conversation and to sell yourself. By selling yourself I don't mean that you beg, plead, and promise to be a hard worker. Selling yourself means that you appear to be charming, entertaining, or otherwise interesting. Once people become interested in you, they'll help you get what you want.

If you can pass the acting tests outlined at the beginning of the book, then you probably have the courage and creativity to become an interesting person. If you're too shy to network, then you can sit in your room all day, practice your monologue, and mail headshots to agents. You might get work this way, but it's more difficult. By networking in the manner that I suggest, you'll be putting yourself in a position to succeed. That's what this plan is all about.

ACTION POINTS

- Networking will speed up your career advancement.
- Networking is nothing more than holding a conversation.
- You can use the power of three to meet anyone you want.
- There are networking opportunities all around you.

DAILY GOALS

Create a section in your acting notebook called "Networking." Within this section, add pages for producers, agents, casting directors, actors, and crew. Try to enter one name per week in one of these categories. Choose one of the networking examples listed in this chapter and go get your first name. If you live in New York or Los Angeles, get to an acting workshop or volunteer for a PA job and you'll soon have a dozen entries.

If you live in a smaller town, go to your local theater and meet the manager and some of the actors there. They will be able to answer your questions and get you to the next step of your acting career.

Finally, find a film festival that you can go to within the next month. You should try that for two reasons. The first is the most obvious: You want to network. Second, while enjoying some original films, you'll be supporting the very artists you wish to join.

With all of the networking ideas I've given you in this chapter, it should be very easy to come up with an answer for your favorite question, "What did you do today to advance your acting career?"

11

ACT NOW!

I'M going to finish up by showing you how to put all these steps together into a regular routine, but first let me be the first to congratulate you on getting this far. By today's standards, reading an entire book puts you into that special category of people who can actually accomplish something that requires intelligence and determination. That's a great sign, because you're going to need those abilities if you're going to make it as an actor. I have a few more very important pieces of information to share with you in this last, short chapter. These should help you put Your Acting Plan into motion.

Continue to work the cycle

Previously I mentioned doing a cycle of mailings, but now it's time to cycle the entire plan. Understanding and executing this step is what separates the actors who just dream about work from those who actually get work. To understand this, let's review the steps of the plan one last time.

1. ***Take the acting tests***—You prove that you have what it takes.
2. ***Learn how to act***—You study and work to get the skills necessary to act.
3. ***Acquire the basics***—You gather the tools necessary to look for auditions.
4. ***Find auditions on your own***—Using the resources provided, you look for acting opportunities for beginners to build experience and credits.
5. ***Contact agents and casting directors***—You promote yourself with casting directors in order to get auditions. You approach agents and ask for representation.
6. ***Work with agents and managers on your career***—You work with your agent and/or manager to get yourself to a higher level of achievement.
7. ***Always be networking***—You constantly build contacts to meet those who can help you.

It's important to know what the daily goals are at each step of the plan so that you're constantly doing things. Remember that "being famous" or even "getting an agent" are not actually things that you can do, those are just things that happen when you're completing your daily goals.

If you're just starting out, you need to challenge yourself to take the acting tests. You can still network while you're doing this, but you're not going to send letters to agents yet. Therefore, your cycle might consist of trying test 3(b) and going to a film festival every month. Those are legitimate activities that you can do to help yourself.

If you're at the end of the plan then your cycle might consist of the following. You go to your acting class every week, look through *Backstage* every Wednesday, and submit yourself for auditions every Thursday. You do mailings to casting directors and agents every Friday. Every Monday night you read publications like *Hollywood Reporter, Premiere,* and your local arts newspaper. You call your agent every Tuesday, and you meet with your college networking group on the last Thursday of each month.

The amount of work that you can do is unlimited. If you're just trying to learn how to act, then maybe you go to an acting workshop one or two nights a week and that's the only thing you do. That's fine as long as you keep doing it. The idea of the cycle means that you know where you are in the plan, and you keep doing the steps that are available to you so that you're always busy and you're always moving forward.

The ideal actor

When conducting interviews for this book, I asked an agent from one of the top five agencies in Los Angeles to describe the ideal type of actor he was looking for. Here's what he said:

> I'd want something like twenty-four years old, handsome, athletic build, and a great actor. Someone who could play the leading man type and the action type. Like a Ben Affleck. A male star like that can survive a bunch of bad movies and still make money. A female star can only endure one or two bad movies.

That man is only one agent at one agency, but he assured me that that type was a prime catch in Hollywood. Actors like Tom Cruise, Mel Gibson, George Clooney, and Vin Diesel all fit into this category, and that's why they are among the highest-paid actors in the world today.

What do you do if you're part of the 99.9 percent of the population that doesn't fit that category? Should you quit? You're not the ideal actor that everyone wants. The good news is that show business takes all types, looks, shapes, and sizes; what really counts is the talent. Look at 4' 11", balding Danny Devito. He's

done pretty well. Look at Arnold Schwarzenegger—a 6' 3"
bodybuilder with a thick Austrian accent. He's done pretty well.
If you let anyone tell you what you can and can't do, then you
are doomed as a creative person. Imagine that Danny Devito had
listened to all the people who told him he was too small or unat-
tractive.

Everyone thinks that only models can work in show business.
Even though there is a great premium put on looks and age, *all*
types are needed in acting. Don't get discouraged if you think
you aren't good-looking enough. You are what you are, and you
can't waste time worrying about it because you have to start
working on your acting career.

"Information" vs. "knowledge"

My mentor, Norman Sturgis, used to talk about information versus knowledge. He said that information was the data we collected from reading books and talking to people, and knowledge
was what we got when we actually did something with the
information. In his classes, he would give us information about
acting, but then he'd make us go up onstage and turn that information into knowledge about acting. You see, it's one thing to
say, "When you're onstage, you have to react to whatever the
other actor says." It's quite another to actually go up onstage and
react to something another actor says.

Norman believed that information by itself was useless, and
only knowledge had any real value. Because you're at the end of
this book, your head is now filled with information about acting.
It's up to you to turn that information into knowledge. The way
you do that is to review each step of Your Acting Plan and then
actually do the steps.

For example, you now have information about how to find an
acting class and practice acting. If you actually find a class and

enroll, then you will gain useful knowledge about the craft of acting. If you never actually practice acting, then your head will remain full of useless information. What then? Will you go buy another acting book? What good will that do if you won't actually put a plan into action? You'll just be filling your head with more and more information.

I have found that the most successful actors I've met in Los Angeles have the fewest acting books. The least successful actors tend to have entire libraries of acting books. They are unsuccessful because they are either untalented or they are simply spending too much time accumulating information and not enough time acquiring knowledge.

Two critical factors

There's a possibility that anybody who reads this book could become a movie star. That doesn't mean that all you have to do is read this book and you'll become famous. I'm just stating that there aren't any laws preventing you from becoming an actor. Anybody who wants to can take a class, get a photo, and look for an agent. Even though I've covered everything you need to know to pursue a career in acting, there are two critical variables that I can't teach you. They are talent and determination.

We all have talents. Some people have a talent for acting. When you become an actor, your talent is that special something that makes people want to look at you, to want to hire you, to want to pay you to act in their productions. I'm not sure if you can learn to be a talented actor, but you can definitely be taught how to expose and utilize the talent that you have. A good acting workshop will provide you with the environment to practice, experiment, and grow as an actor. If you do that on a regular basis, then your true talent will come out. Only then will you discover what kind of an actor you are.

The second variable is determination, that is, the courage to act on your desire, to actually do something. It sounds very trite to say, "If you want to become an actor then go act in something," yet that's really what it comes down to, and that's why I've repeated that theme throughout this book. If you don't have the desire and courage to follow these steps, then there's nothing I can say to make you do it. If you need someone to pump you up and motivate you, then you have no chance of becoming an actor. It's hard enough to do it when you're very passionate about it. If you're lazy about it, then it's almost impossible.

So those are the two unknown variables—talent and determination. Each is worthless without the other. When you put those two variables together though, great things can happen as long as you keep trying. Here are two examples of actors who were once in the same position as you. That is, they were not popular types or well-known actors. They came from small towns and fought incredible odds and obstacles to make it. Let them inspire you.

America Ferrera

America Ferrera is female, Hispanic, and overweight. You can't get much different from Julia Roberts. America is an eighteen-year-old Honduran actor who is getting a lot of buzz after winning this year's Special Jury Prize for Acting as Lead Actress at the Sundance Film Festival. The film she starred in is a Spanish-language independent called *Real Women Have Curves*. It was America's second film credit. It was a low-budget independent, just like one of the many films that you could audition for.

America Ferrera is suddenly in the news and on the entertainment magazine pages. I've seen her on TV twice this week and I'm reading about her in one of LA's newspapers. How is that possible? She's a heavy, Hispanic female. Here's what America had to say about her attempt to become an actor:

I never had the support of my family, or anyone telling me, "You can do it, you can make it." More often than not I heard how impossible it was, and my mom tried to direct me toward education instead.

If I didn't know better, I'd think that that quote was one of the hundreds of e-mails I receive on a regular basis. No one supported her. Everyone said she was crazy. This is typical of how people are treated when they tell someone they want to become an actor. But America believed in herself and her abilities, and her hard work and dedication paid off.

Nia Vardalos

The week that I write this marks another milestone for this year's biggest hit movie, *My Big Fat Greek Wedding*. Made for $5 million, this film has now grossed more than $200 million to become the most profitable independent film to date. The Hollywood papers and TV stations are constantly running stories about this film and its star, Nia Vardalos.

Nia's story has become a legend in just one year. A struggling Canadian actor, considered too old for mainstream Hollywood, she wrote and acted in a one-woman play called *My Big Fat Greek Wedding* at a small theater in Hollywood. In the audience one night was Rita Wilson, an actress and producer who just happened to be married to Tom Hanks. Rita, whose family is half Greek, loved the play and talked to Nia about a film script. Nia, prepared actress that she is, had a script ready to go. Rita Wilson produced the film and Nia starred in it.

This film is one of those rare gems that keeps getting more and more popular because people truly love it. It hasn't slowed down and now there is a TV show based on the film, starring Nia Vardalos as the lead. It's possible that by the time this book comes out, that TV show might have flopped or become a big hit. Whatever happens to it is irrelevant and won't diminish Nia's accomplishment. Nia, by the way, is not your typical leading lady type.

America and Nia succeeded because they had the courage and determination to give it a shot. It's that simple. America stated very clearly that her mother discouraged her. Even though her mother told her not to try, she did it anyway and succeeded. And what about Nia? Doesn't she know that if you're a forty-year-old female, Canadian actor, you aren't allowed to succeed? Doesn't she know that only Julia Roberts and Ben Affleck types can get work in Hollywood?

Do you know what Nia's secret was? If you don't, then reread this book. I'll give you a hint: She learned to act, she took some photos, she got into a play, and she networked like crazy and put herself into a position to succeed. Does that sound familiar to you yet?

That is the kind of determination you need. Nia had to spend many days at home writing her play and her movie. She could've been out at the beach or playing video games, but instead she chose to sit down and write a play. I can't teach you how to have that kind of dedication. All I can say is that you'll need it if you want to succeed. If you have some talent, like America and Nia obviously do, and if you find the courage within your heart to actually follow the steps of Your Acting Plan, you're going to put yourself in the best possible position to succeed. These two women are living proof that it can be done even if you aren't exactly what Hollywood is looking for.

It truly doesn't matter where you come from or what you look like. If you have the talent and determination, you can find a place in show business. I'm not saying that it's easy, because it isn't. Becoming an actor just might be one of the most difficult career paths you could possibly choose. I hear too many actors say they can't make it for stupid reasons like poverty, skin color, or looks. No matter what your situation is, there have been actors who were poorer than you when they started. There are actors who have the same skin color as you. There are actors who aren't as good-looking as you. Stop using those excuses.

Most famous actors reached stardom the exact same way—they did whatever was available to them at the time. They also never gave up and eventually one production led to another and they worked their way up. They all took slightly different roads, but they used the same map.

If you could call your favorite actors and ask them how they got started, they wouldn't say things like, "Actually it was very easy. One day an agent called me up and asked me if I wanted to be a movie star." Instead, Jim Carrey might tell you about how his elementary school teacher used to let him perform a routine at the start of each class. Charlize Theron might tell you that the first thing she did was take ballet lessons in South Africa. Benicio Del Toro might tell you about how he dropped out of college to study acting with legendary teacher Stella Adler in Los Angeles. Halle Berry might tell you about the time she entered her first beauty pageant in her home state of Ohio.

You're going to start the exact same way that all those stars began their careers. You're going to do the first thing that's available to you right now. That might be a local acting workshop, a school play, a student video, a beauty pageant, or talking to your pets out on the back porch. You're going to do something because you have this burning, insatiable drive to become an actor. If you have this drive, then nothing is going to stop you. It won't matter where you start, and it really won't matter who takes your headshot or how you format your résumé. Nothing will stand in your way if you have true talent and the determination to fulfill your desire to be an actor.

You can lead a horse to water but you can't make him drink

That's a wonderful cliché and one that is completely appropriate for the way I feel about you right now. You have in your hands a book that tells you everything you need to know about how to become an actor. Oh, sure, you could search the Internet and read other books and find a few details that I might have left out or didn't explain clearly enough. No book covers every single thing perfectly. However, I've given you more than enough. If you don't succeed, it won't be because you didn't have enough "information."

If you follow these steps, you aren't going to suddenly stall because the steps are wrong. You're not going to call me and say, "Hey Pete, remember what you said about sending letters? It's all wrong. Hollywood just changed the rules and you can't send letters to agents anymore." That's not going to happen.

This is your map. This is the water of your success. Are you going to drink it? I can't make you. Your parents, spouse, girlfriend, boyfriend, teacher, or dog can't make you do anything. I can't make you move to New York, share an apartment, work as a bartender, and study acting in the afternoons. I can't make you call up a headshot photographer and get a picture taken. I can't make you sit home on a Saturday night and write letters to agents. I can't make you spend your Thanksgiving weekend in a cold field in Minnesota shooting a film that nobody will ever see so that you can get a credit on your résumé. Nobody can make you do any of these things. Only you can do that.

Many will suggest that you write your goals down on paper. Write down "I'm going to become an actor" on a piece of paper and stick it on your head. What good will that do? You already know you want to become an actor; you don't have to be reminded. Even if you wrote that down and looked at it every day, how will you find the strength to actually do something?

I don't know the answer to that. Nobody knows the answer to that. All I can say is that if you have that strength, then you will pursue your goals and you'll turn your information into knowledge. If you don't have it, then you'll just keep reading books and searching for shortcuts on websites.

If you only learn one thing from this book, I hope you learn that nothing is as important as continually trying. As long as you're doing something, then nothing else will really matter. An actor once asked me to give him just one piece of advice. He wanted to know what the one thing was that would help him the most in becoming an actor. I asked him this question, "What did you do today to advance your acting career?"

Appendix A

INTERNET SCAMS

The two most common reasons that actors get scammed on the Internet is because they don't understand the casting process, and they want things to happen quickly. Many website designers know this, and they're going to prey on your dreams as they take your money. Before you pay for any acting-related product on the Internet, I want you to check for certain red flags and ask yourself what it is you think you're paying for.

Warning signs that you're about to be scammed

- Claims of instant success
- Guarantees for auditions for TV shows or major movies
- Promises of getting discovered by agents or casting directors
- Offers that feature expensive portfolios
- Anything vague

When you see these it's usually time to exit that site; otherwise, your money will be exiting from your pocket and you'll get scammed.

Instant Success

Avoid the "instant success" model. Beginners often refuse to believe that acting success comes through hard work, dedication, and years of persistence. So if you ever see a website that leads you to think that you are going to succeed or get discovered just by joining the site, and not doing anything else, then you're probably being misled. You can't just join some website and become an actor.

Once again, here's the whole process in a nutshell. Learn to act, keep training, build credits on your own, get an agent, build credits with the help of your agent, and on and on. It never ends. That's the whole cycle. No website can replace that process. You can't just go from wanting to be an actor to being a superstar by clicking your mouse and paying a fee.

Auditions for TV shows or major movies

As you learned in the casting process, the casting directors for TV shows, major movies, and most commercials send audition notices through the breakdowns to the legitimate agents. Casting directors for these types of productions don't post their auditions on the Internet, and they're usually only available to actors who live in Los Angeles and New York. So any site that tells you that you can audition for a major TV show or movie is misleading you because that's not how casting works.

Most of the auditions available online are for student films and videos, independent films, theater, and other similar projects. Although lots of legitimate auditions can be found online and some will pay wages, I'm trying to warn you against the sites that mislead you into thinking you'll be getting auditions for network TV shows or major motion pictures. You will not.

Getting discovered by agents or casting directors

As you've learned by now, casting directors and talent agents are constantly being approached by actors looking for work, and they also have their network of contacts who bring them promising leads. That's why they do not search the Internet looking for actors.

If you find a site that says "Get discovered" or "Get seen by agents and casting directors," then you should probably exit from that website regardless of how they claim to do this. Once again, you're being misled. Some of these companies claim to send your portfolio to the casting directors in the form of a CD, book, or link to your portfolio. Don't waste your money on this. Casting directors will see your photo if you mail it to them with a résumé and cover letter. I've already explained how to do that earlier in the book.

Expensive portfolios

Typically anything expensive, especially an online portfolio, is usually a rip-off. Don't be fooled by these companies and their hired "scouts." The *scout* is another word for *high-pressure sales rep,* whom these companies hire to sell online portfolios to beginners. They'll put up beautiful pictures and success stories on their sites, and then they'll tell you to pay a large fee so that you can get a nice portfolio and start getting auditions. They don't care where you live, what you look like, or anything else. They just want your money.

I've had numerous scouts from these companies contact me and tell me that they had no experience or training as talent scouts. They were just hired and told to sell a certain number of portfolios a week to meet their quota. They want you to think that this online portfolio will be seen by lots of important people, but the reality is that it will probably be seen by you and your family members and nobody else.

It's always good to have a headshot and résumé online, but you can do it for free or very cheaply at reputable sites like www.backstage.com, www.therightcast.com, and many others. Good companies like these will encourage you to post a head-shot and résumé online to aid in your networking; they won't mislead you with the promise of "getting discovered."

Anything vague

If you can't tell exactly what the site does or what will happen when you join or buy, then you have no business paying for any-thing. If it claims to list auditions without specifically stating the auditions, then you should be concerned. If a site says that you're going to be discovered in some way that isn't clearly explained, then it's time to leave. Always remember as you begin to fill out a form or pay for something to ask yourself, why am I doing this? What do I think is going to happen?

I'm always amazed when actors e-mail me and say, "Pete, can you please check out this website and tell me if it's a scam or not? I can't tell what it is they do." Forget about whether or not it's a scam. If you can't tell what it does, then why pay money? That's a sign that you're looking for the easy route. That route doesn't exist.

Some websites have you fill out a form and pay a fee as one of the first steps of the process. Or you just fill out the form and then you get an e-mail later asking you to pay some kind of fee. Be very careful about these, and always ask yourself what you're paying for.

What should I pay for exactly?

As an actor, you'll need to get headshots, and you'll need to enroll in an ongoing class. That's about it. If you live in a major market, then consider joining a site like www.backstage.com or www.therightcast.com. They'll charge you a low monthly fee, and they'll send you listings of legitimate auditions for mostly independent projects. If you don't live in a major market, then try to find a free casting service that covers your area. Other than that, you don't really need to pay for much. Therefore, any website that charges you a large fee, makes claims of success or discovery, or otherwise leads you to think that the whole acting process can be circumvented by paying a fee is probably not a wise investment.

I don't want you to think that you should never pay for anything on the Internet or that every acting website or product is a scam. That's not true at all. Before I wrote this book I used to sell a lot of this information through my website. That's just honest business, and there are plenty of people who sell legitimate products and services to actors. I've made friends with many in the online acting community who have good products and good intentions.

I want you to use the information in this section as a guide to help you make an informed decision. As a consumer of anything, your best defense against rip-offs is education.

Appendix B

NOBODY NEEDS A UNION CARD

There is a great misunderstanding among beginning actors that getting a union card, specifically the SAG card, will somehow unlock the doors of show business. Nothing could be further from the truth. It's not that the union card isn't good to have, because it is. What isn't good is spending all your time worrying about how to get one. Here's the big secret that most beginners don't realize. Nobody needs a union card.

"Pete, how on earth can you say that nobody needs a union card? I've always been told that you can't work without one." Take a moment to think about how crazy that statement is. If you can't work without a union card, then how did Al Pacino get work? How did Reese Witherspoon get work? Do you know that *The Mask* was Cameron Diaz's first movie?

One of the biggest misconceptions about working as an actor is that you can't get work if you're not in the union. The union of course is the Screen Actors Guild, commonly known as SAG. There are other unions for actors, but SAG is the the main union because it governs film production, and the SAG card is considered the Holy Grail for beginners who think that it will bring them fame and fortune. What these beginners don't realize is that it's not necessary to have a SAG card to audition for SAG movies. In addition, simply having a SAG card is no guarantee of work and, in some cases, might actually hurt a beginner.

Why you don't need a SAG card to get a role in a SAG movie

In 1947, Congress passed the Taft-Hartley Labor Act, which regulated labor relations. Among the provisions of the act was a clause that outlawed the "closed shop." In a closed shop, employees had to join the union before being eligible for employment with the unionized employer. What this means to actors is that you do not have to join the union to audition for or work in a union film. If you get a role in a union film, you can work for up to thirty days before you have to join the union. After the thirty days, you must join the union if you want to work on a union production again. That's not a loophole or a trick, it's a fact of working in show business, and you can find that information on the SAG website, www.sag.org.

The card comes to you when you're ready

A SAG card is not something that is obtained as a prerequisite for work. It's something that comes to you when you need it. In other words, if you keep following the steps of Your Acting Plan, then you'll keep auditioning for independent films, student films, commercials, and other low-budget stuff. You'll start out doing free work for students and community theaters. Once you have enough experience, you'll get an agent, and that agent will send you on auditions for better roles. You don't need a union card to do that. One day your agent gets you an audition for some type of union shoot. You'll go to the audition even though you're not a member of SAG. If they choose you and you get cast, you will then be eligible to join the union and you'll get your SAG card. That's how it works.

I can't count the number of people who've e-mailed me saying that they want to come to Los Angeles but they want to get their SAG card first. This is a complete waste of time. If they were asked how they got their SAG card, most professional actors would probably tell you that they got cast in a film or commercial that was SAG, so they became SAG. Did you get that? Here it is again. They weren't SAG. Then they got cast in a SAG production, and they became a member of SAG.

No actor ever lost a role because she wasn't a member of SAG

In the chapter on the casting process, I stated that casting directors are always trying to find the best possible talent for each role. They don't care if you're in the union or not, they just need the best actor they can find. Remember that once you get into an audition, everyone is equal. That is, once the casting director says "action," you have to prove yourself with your acting abilities. If you're good enough, you'll get the part and nobody will care about your union status. As you search for auditions, don't be discouraged if you see a casting notice that says "SAG." That doesn't mean you have to be in SAG to audition. It only means that you might have to join SAG if you get the role.

A union card is worthless on its own

Imagine if I were able to break into the offices of SAG and enter your name into their computer as a union member. Then I printed out a card and handed it to you. What would happen? What would you do next? Would you all of a sudden start getting auditions? Would agents start calling you? The only thing that would change is that you'll now be expected to pay your yearly dues, and you won't be able to work in all the nonunion opportunities that can help build your résumé and experience. That's because SAG has something called "Rule One," which states that once you're in SAG, you won't do any nonunion work. You're worse off.

Some agents say that they only work with "union" talent

I've heard actors complain that an agent turned them down because they weren't in the union. Once again, they erroneously think it's because of that physical card. It's not.

Agents understand the process described in Your Acting Plan, and they know that the union card is not something that is magically obtained. It's something that comes to you when you've been working hard in the film business for a few years and building experience. If you don't have a union card, it usually means that you're either a beginner or that you're not a very good actor. Most agents don't want beginners or bad actors; therefore, they say, "I don't work with nonunion actors." It's a screening process.

For the last time, stop worrying about the SAG card. I'm not saying that it isn't good to have one. It's a strong union with good benefits. All I'm saying is that you shouldn't put all your energy into trying to get that card. If you keep following the steps of Your Acting Plan, then the SAG card will come to you when you're ready.

Appendix C

EXTRA WORK

Extras are those nonspeaking actors needed to fill scenes around the principal actors. I highly recommend doing extra work as a way to make a little bit of money, network, get involved, and see the business up close. There's also an outside chance that you could get a SAG card out of it.

How to do it

In large markets you can sign up with an extras casting agency. You'll possibly pay a registration fee and a low monthly fee. These are considered legitimate fees. Once you join the service, you'll be able to call in daily and ask for assignments. You can also hire a calling-in service to make these calls for you. If the agency has a project for your type, you'll be told where and when to go. You'll report to that location, and you'll be given a voucher that is proof that you worked. Plan on being there for at least twelve hours.

In a small market, there might not be enough work to support an extras casting service. If this is the case, then check with your state's film commission website or check with the local casting director about getting work.

How much money do I make as an extra?

On a typical twelve-hour union movie shoot, you can expect to make about $100. That number could go as high as $600 or more depending on factors too numerous to mention here.

Can you really get a SAG card by doing extra work?

Yes, you can, but don't count on it and don't worry about it. If you're on a union shoot and the director asks you to say a line on camera, then you automatically get bumped up from an extra to a "principal" or "day player." You will get a higher rate of pay, and you'll then be eligible to join the union.

The second way to do it is to collect union vouchers. SAG rules state that a certain number of extras have to be union extras. If not enough union actors choose to work on a film as extras, then they have to hand out the union vouchers to nonunion extras. It happens frequently. If you collect three union vouchers, you can then join the union.

Resources for finding extra work

These resources provide you with absolutely everything you need to know about working as an extra. The books will pay for themselves because you'll get work instantly.

Websites

- www.billdancecasting.com
- www.ep-services.com
- www.extrascastingguild.com
- www.backtoone.net

Books

- *Extra Work for Brain Surgeons*—This pocket guide lists services, rates, tips, and everything else needed to find work.
- *Movie Extra Work for Rocket Scientists*—This is a more comprehensive resource that clearly explains every facet of extra work and also provides all the contact information for the various services in Los Angeles.
- *Back to One*—This is another outstanding resource for learning everything about extra work and how to get started.

INDEX